796.358

cc
Ca

AUTHOR	CLASS
KAY, J.	W126

TITLE	No.
Lancashire	491206259

A History of County Cricket

LANCASHIRE

A History of County Cricket

LANCASHIRE

John Kay

Arthur Barker Limited
5 Winsley Street London W1

ISBN 0 213 16405 1

Printed in Great Britain by
Bristol Typesetting Co Ltd, Barton Manor, St Philips, Bristol

Contents

For Jane and Jonathan

Illustrations

David Hughes, another promising Lancashire all-rounder
J. D. Bond, the Lancashire Captain
The semi-final of the 1971 Gillette Cup

between pages 136 and 137

The 1971 Lancashire team with the Gillette Cup
Jack Bond and Farokh Engineer after their victory
The 1971 Lancashire staff and team
T. A. Higson, Major Rupert Howard, Cedric S. Rhoades
 and Bert Flack

Acknowledgements
The author and publishers would like to thank the following for permission to reproduce the photographs in this book: the management and library of the Lancashire County Cricket Club: Sport and General Press Agency Ltd.; Central Press Photos Ltd.; Hallawell Photos; Bert Butterworth; The *Guardian* and the *Manchester Evening News*.

Introduction

All is well with Lancashire cricket! After years in the doldrums, without a major cricketing honour for more than thirty years, the Red Rose is now in full bloom. The Gillette Cup has been won twice in succession, the John Player League championship has gone to Old Trafford for two successive years, and the crowds are back again. With success on the field has come a revival of enthusiasm around the ring, and for the first time in years the 1971 season offered positive proof that things are going well with the announcement of a record five-figure profit. Such is the state of affairs at Old Trafford today. Jack Bond leads an attractive and enthusiastic team on the field. Cedric Rhoades sets a similar example of enterprise and energy in the committee room, and Secretary Jack Wood is proving that a Yorkshireman has much to offer Lancashire in the way of plain sound common-sense administration. It is true that the most important cricketing honour of them all, the county championship, yet eludes this new-look Lancashire side. But the team Bond leads so well has finished third from the top these last two seasons and such is the power and promise of the side that success in this field should not be beyond reach in the near future.

It has taken something of a cricketing miracle, on and off the field, to restore the bloom to the Red Rose county. In 1964, the club's centenary year, things could not have been worse. Playing results were dreadful. The players endured rather than enjoyed their cricket. The committee were apparently content to drift casually on, relying upon membership and the financial assistance of prominent officials. Old Trafford was a sporting ghost-spot. There was no lack of good players produced in the area, but lots of them bypassed the county headquarters in their determination to achieve cricketing respectability – and those who did throw in their lot at Old Trafford soon lost their appetite for the game. Even worse, in the towns and the leagues scattered all over a wide shire there was precious little regard for Lancashire from the cricketing point of view. Saturday afternoon players openly scoffed at the feeble efforts of their so-called betters in the first-class sphere and although there was, on the face of things, a respectable relationship between county and leagues on an administrative level, there was no real cooperation.

In a word Lancashire County Cricket Club were content to live in the past. No opportunity was ever missed to pay tribute to the players and officials of old. The golden days of Archie MacLaren, the Hornbys, Reggie Spooner and Johnny Briggs were often cited as imperishable cricketing memories. The attitude of those in charge was one of the 'private club' atmosphere. They wanted the privilege of exclusiveness and none of the criticisms so often levelled at sporting bodies presenting a public spectacle. It could not go on, and it did not! A group of members grew tired of the long, dreary years in the wilderness. They saw mistakes made and lessons unlearned, good young players came from the leagues, full of talent and enthusiasm, to become mere cricketing robots in next to no time. While they watched and wondered, many members resigned, taking the easy way out. At annual meetings they had been rebuffed time and time again in their efforts to obtain information or inaugurate new standards. They knew that the relationship between players on the one side, and committee on the other, was drifting further and further apart. And towards the end of the 1964 season Cedric Rhoades, a young Manchester textile merchant, who had played a little league cricket and helped to administer it at club level, took the initiative. He organised a petition expressing concern and alarm at the way things were drifting, and in a matter of weeks he had more than enough support to demand a special general meeting and propose a vote of censure on those then in charge.

It was an unfortunate state of affairs and an undignified one. But it was also a necessary prelude to the reorganisation so earnestly needed if Lancashire cricket was to be rescued. The club secretary resigned and Jack Wood was appointed his successor. He arrived in the heat of the controversy and sat in at the special general meeting when lots of dirty linen was washed in public and many old-time members shook their heads in despair. Many resigned, sadly disillusioned and completely alienated by the action of the so-called rebels in forcing a showdown. They were not rebels in any manner of speaking. Cedric Rhoades led a bunch of cricket lovers who had seen their beloved county sink down to the depths, and they were determined it should not stay there. They carried their vote of censure easily, and the committee of the day resigned *en bloc*, though with one or two exceptions offering themselves for re-election. Six succeeded in retaining their places but six new men, with the enterprising Mr Rhoades at the top of the poll, joined them and the new deal began. An archaic rule permitting vice-presidents the power of a veto at committee meetings was abolished and Lancashire cricket became democratic. It was slow going at first and one or two new members of the committee, lacking patience and tolerance, resigned because things were not moving fast enough. Cedric Rhoades remained and in due course stepped into the chair.

Rhoades was the youngest man ever appointed to such a responsible position, but he had the confidence both of the members and the players, and Lancashire's improvement stemmed from this key appointment. Finance was a tremendous barrier. An overdraft at the bank and a debt to a vice-president were like millstones round a dying club's neck and the new chairman had to get his priorities right. He enthusiastically supported a revolutionary project to hive off parts of the vast Old Trafford enclosures that were not directly concerned with cricket. The plan was to develop the car parks fronting the pavilion on Talbot Road into office blocks and even a restaurant and hotel. The land lay idle eight months of the year and the upkeep was crippling. It was sound economic planning but it broke with tradition and angered many of the elderly members who feared their comfort was in danger. Mr Rhoades was not the pioneer of this scheme but he was the man who steered it eloquently through an annual meeting with a promise that should the first stage of the three planned rebuilding schemes be successful the club retained the right to withdraw from the last two. An annual income of some

£90,000 was envisaged. And it was achieved with the completion of the first phase, an undertaking achieved by a masterly piece of planning and architectural delicacy. Office blocks were built and rented without blotting the Old Trafford landscape, and the towering blocks bore the names of distinguished cricketers, Mac-Laren, Statham and Washbrook among them!

Building the offices was one thing. Once accomplished there came an opportunity to sell them at a price bringing financial security for the foreseeable future. The opportunity was taken and the rest of the three-phase plan abandoned. Relieved of financial burden, attention was turned to the playing side and Lancashire wholeheartedly campaigned for the limited introduction of overseas players into the county championship in an effort to attract a still only mildly interested public back to Old Trafford. Determined to rebuild Lancashire cricket with Lancashire material, the committee wanted time to reorganize the pipe line from the schools to the county staff, and although they were outbid for the services of Gary Sobers they signed Farokh Engineer and Clive Lloyd to plug the most glaring gaps until they could train their own young players. It was a break with tradition and an alleged offence to the memory of old-time 'greats' in some eyes. Yet it was sound cricketing logic and with the appointment, first of Brian Statham and then of Jack Bond, as captain, off-the-field security was burnished with on-the-field sparkle. The Gillette Cup competition and the John Player league were tailor-made for the players Bond led. They tasted success in his first year, and liked it. Five matches in a row were won and they signposted the road back. One-day cricket was Lancashire's salvation. Lloyd and Engineer were happily merged into the side. Under Bond the team regained its appetite, and, happily married to the committee and officials instead of unhappily divorced, the fight back was accomplished the simple way.

Bond insisted that his players enjoy their cricket. He, like many of his own generation, was not too happy about sacrificing three-day standards, but he saw the necessity for it. 'We may not like the new style but if it brings back the crowds it will serve its purpose', was the gist of his orders. His men accepted them, and went out to enjoy themselves, finding the secret of entertaining at the same time. In three years they won back the ground that had been lost in thirty. Old Trafford is no longer a sporting ghost-spot. Lancashire is the game's new trend-setter and the story of how it was all accomplished makes fascinating reading. There is still much hard work ahead. Nobody believes otherwise. When Bond goes a new captain will have to be found and perhaps new ideals established. This is a changing world and cricket cannot afford to ignore it. A county club with a golden heritage was allowed to drift to the point of ridicule and near extinction because the past was regarded as more important than the future. The same mistake will not be made again. Lancashire cricket is thriving once again; it must and will remain that way!

Creative response to the secular world

Part One

From the beginnings to the second world war

I. THE FORMATIVE YEARS

In the very beginning, Lancashire cricket was Manchester cricket. There is ample evidence that way back in the early days of the nineteenth century cricket flourished in and around the Manchester area, and the Manchester club itself can trace its origin back to 1818; even then records suggest the club had been in existence for several years, because it had won esteem and appreciation from all who played or watched a noble game. The Manchester club played its first games in Salford, at the Crescent, and later moved to Moss Lane in Hulme which was then a select residential district of the city and a place where life proceeded at a leisurely gait. One of the earliest score books still in existence gives details of a match between Manchester and a Garrison team. Manchester, it is disclosed, enjoyed the aid of French, a Liverpool professional, and the Garrison opposition was made up of soldiers from the Coldstream Guards and the Queen's Bays; one man was given out ' foot before wicket '. The Garrison also employed professional aid in the person of Carter, also from Liverpool, but neither he nor French made much of an impression in a low-scoring match left drawn because of rain. Thus, one is led to believe, began the legend, often far from true, that Manchester, cricket, and rain are synonymous.

By 1842 Manchester's cricketers were looking further afield for matches. They had earned and enjoyed the privilege of playing against neighbouring clubs and were ambitious to try their skill against rivals from outside areas. An invitation was received and accepted to send a side to Lord's to play the Gentlemen of the MCC but the northerners were outclassed and actually gave

18

up the game after the MCC had bowled their visitors out for a meagre fifty-nine and replied with two hundred. Judging by a faded newspaper cutting it was Manchester's attack that failed to rise to the occasion, although a modest fifty-nine hardly suggests the batsmen were in top form. ' The bowling on the part of Manchester was very deficient, it being of the old-fashioned under-hand school, which afforded the Marylebone gentlemen much amusement in hitting away ', says the scribe. He certainly made a valid point. Round-arm bowling had been legal since 1828 and Manchester's cricketers were obviously way behind the times in their first venture at cricket's hallowed headquarters. Yet the beaten side were far from downcast. They returned home sadder, perhaps, but also much wiser, and were soon ready for a new challenge. Two years later they met and defeated an all-Yorkshire team in the course of a rebuilding period when far more matches were won than lost, and during which the cult of round-arm bowling was ' well and thoroughly ' accepted as the new order of things.

By 1847, Manchester, predominantly all amateur but never averse to recruiting ' specialized ' assistance for important games, were ready to challenge a touring all-England side that included the great George Parr. The newcomer, one of the game's earliest giants, was obviously a batsman to be respected. He hit a century at Leicester and seventy-eight not out at York before delighting the Manchester members and players with an innings of sixty-four. His prowess was such that another faded newspaper cutting of the day, describing his batsmanship as 'masterly', also suggested that the men of Manchester might ' heed with advantage the ease with which Parr made his strokes and the manner in which he challenged the bowlers by fleetness of foot and assurance of eye '. Thus were the cardinal virtues of batsmanship laid down for the benefit of those that followed. Observation of the same principles today would be of lasting benefit still.

Gathering strength, and displaying increasing authority and ability on the field, it was not long before the Manchester club again moved ground. This time Old Trafford was the chosen spot, but not the Old Trafford we know today. The first site, situated on Chester Road, was then known as the Botanical Gardens, and is now the White City Greyhound Stadium, and by 1849 there was sufficient interest and confidence in the Manchester ranks to issue a challenge to Yorkshire. It was accepted and the first match took place at Sheffield, with the return at Old Trafford, two years later Yorkshire visiting Old Trafford again. The battle of the cricketing roses had been established and although Lancashire, not then officially in existence, does not rate these encounters as official, Yorkshire certainly does. Across the Pennines Manchester and Lancashire were synonymous in cricket and no distinction was ever drawn by those with White Rose affiliations.

It was these meetings between the might of Yorkshire and the pride of Manchester that ultimately led to talk of expansion and the eventual formation of the Lancashire County and Manchester Cricket Club. In 1857 Manchester tested their strength once again in a match against a powerful Surrey side. Strengthened by the inclusion of three professionals, Wisden, Lillywhite and Davies, Manchester won a thrilling encounter by three runs on the Western Club ground at Eccles; it was the only defeat sustained by the strong southern side in ten fixtures.

Although there is no confirmation, it is possible that this game, played on 3, 4 and 5 September 1857, was Manchester's last three-day engagement before a move was made to the present ground at Old Trafford. The move was forced upon the club by the loss of the Botanical Gardens site to an Arts and Treasures Exhibition and despite a keen and often bitter battle to preserve the ground for cricket, eviction was threatened and the new site chosen. Within almost a six hit the alternative spot was discovered; it had already been used for cricket 'by miscellaneous groups of gentlemen eager to enjoy themselves in the summertime'.

Be that as it may, Manchester moved in and the official opening, in June 1857, was accompanied by a cricketing battle between Manchester and Liverpool, rivals on the field but always willing cooperators in the cause of cricket when county cricket became officially established. When Manchester first occupied Old Trafford the ground consisted of eight acres of 'good, level and sandy land, with a pavilion erected on the north side'. This building, apparently not regarded as any great ornament to the surroundings, consisted of a centre compartment (intended for a dining hall) and two wings with a turret surmounting the centre. Its main hall was 36 feet long and 22 feet wide and underneath was an excellent wine cellar and a residence for the then club professional, one Thomas Hunt, a Yorkshireman whose wife was responsible for the cleanliness of the pavilion. Considering that the dining hall had giant windows to provide vantage points for watching play, her task was by no means an easy one. Nevertheless she obviously carried out her duties satisfactorily, for upon the death of her husband she was granted a benefit match on the ground, undoubtedly the first of many to enrich Lancashire cricketers then unborn. The removal from the old ground to the new, it is recorded, cost Manchester £1,000. It was undoubtedly a lot of money in those far-off days, but who can doubt it was cheap at the price?

The new Old Trafford got away to an auspicious start. Liverpool were beaten by thirty-one runs, being twice dismissed for under a hundred, and there followed matches against Broughton, Sheffield and Shrewsbury. Soon a new pavilion became essential and was built at a cost of £900, the beginning of the present impressive structure, Surrey being invited to Manchester to mark the official opening ceremony. The southerners were beaten. In the Manchester side were two members of the Rowley family, a name that was to mean much when, after a game with an all-England side at Broughton, it was decided that the time had come to establish a county club and side. The first steps to expansion were taken at a meeting held in the Queen's Hotel, Manchester, on 12 January 1864, and after 'a thorough discussion of the possibilities and desirability of spreading a thorough knowledge and appreciation of the game throughout Lancashire' it was unanimously decided to form a County Cricket Club. The meeting attracted a sizeable gathering of amateur cricketers from all parts of the county, and it was agreed that matches should be played in Manchester, Preston, Liverpool, Blackburn, 'and other places where interest was manifest'. The annual subscription of founder members was resolved at one guinea and it was agreed that any profit made should be funded to secure and maintain a ground that would do the club credit and answer all the cricketing requirements of the county.

Among the Manchester club representatives at the meeting were the already mentioned E. B. Rowley and his brother A. B. Rowley, and S. H. Swire, names that were to figure prominently in the annals of Lancashire cricket. Other Manchester area clubs were well represented and interested parties travelled from Liverpool, Blackburn, Oldham and Wigan. They all agreed that Old Trafford should be the headquarters of the new club but they wanted fixtures to be spread around the county area. In June of the same year Lancashire played their first ever truly representative match when Birkenhead Park were opposed by an all-amateur team at Warrington on the fifteenth and sixteenth of that month. Records, alas, do not name the first man to captain the county but with S. H. Swire and the two Rowleys in the side one would doubt any desire to go outside these three stalwarts for leadership purposes. Certainly A. B. Rowley shone with the bat, hitting fifty-seven in the first innings when one B. J. Lawrence took eight opposition wickets to give the county a lead of twenty-six. A second innings collapse for seventy-eight saw the game slipping away but the Park were held, although reaching 90-1 before time was called.

In the return encounter, at Birkenhead Park, Lancashire called up three professionals, Hickton, Holgate and Nicholls, but a heavy-scoring game was drawn and the club completed the 1864 season with all-amateur sides opposing the Gentlemen of Shropshire, Warwickshire and Yorkshire, travelling to Warwick, Shrewsbury and York in the process and entertaining their rivals at Liverpool, Old Trafford and Broughton, thus fulfilling the founding desire to play matches over a wide area. The first ever county engagement followed in 1865 when Middlesex were opposed at Old Trafford, and although Lancashire won by sixty-two runs after a tie on the first innings there could be no denying that a Middlesex player was the 'man of the match', even if the phrase was then unknown. V. E. Walker, a member of a famous Southgate cricketing family, took all ten Lancashire wickets in the second innings and for the return encounter at Islington, Lancashire again enlisted professional aid but were beaten by ten wickets, despite the inclusion of Roger Iddison, a Yorkshireman, and Fred Reynolds, two paid players whose names are prominent in the early history of Lancashire cricket. At the end of the 1865 season there could be no doubting the success and the importance of the new county club. It had been successfully launched and although Old Trafford was still officially the Manchester club ground the two bodies merged instinctively; what was good for one was also good for the other, although as the years rolled by the growing public who watched and played cricket began to look upon the club as purely and simply Lancashire. Officially it was never so, and it was almost a century later before the Manchester club officially ceased to be linked with the Lancashire one. And even today there are old-timers who still insist that Lancashire cricket was essentially Manchester cricket in the very beginning.

2. THE GOOD WORK CONTINUES

From 1866 to 1872 Lancashire contented themselves with a modest fixture list. Four inter-county games highlighted the 1866 season and Manchester's part in the scheme of things to be was steadfastly observed with a series of club matches wisely 'inserted' among the first-class fixtures. In addition to Middlesex, Surrey were met, and so were an MCC and Ground side from Lord's. Yorkshire, of course, were met both home and away and it is recorded that during the same season four Hornby brothers played for the Gentlemen of Cheshire against the Gentlemen of Lancashire. Three weeks later two of the talented brothers A. N. and E. K., were playing for Lancashire against Yorkshire and opening up a family connection that brought much lustre to both players and club, spreading from the playing field to the committee room and bearing an influence far beyond estimation. Slowly but surely Lancashire expanded their cricketing ambitions and fixture list. Nottinghamshire, Sussex, Hampshire, Derbyshire and Kent were met in championship matches and although Lancashire had to wait until 1879 before they won honour by tying with Nottinghamshire for the title, their reputation as formidable cricketing foes was growing. Rules and regulations were loosely worded and casually implemented in the nineteenth century and although Iddison had played for Lancashire, in 1865 he returned to Yorkshire, only to appear again at Old Trafford as a Lancashire professional. And to him goes the credit of hitting the county's first century, a memorable 106 against Surrey at the Oval. A year later, one James Ricketts carried his bat for Lancashire, hitting 195 on his début. To this day no batsman has started his career with Lancashire to better effect, but Ricketts, although he played county cricket for ten years, never fully realised the promise of his remarkable début.

The 1867 season started on a doleful note for Lancashire. They played Yorkshire three times, at Old Trafford, Whalley and Middlesborough, and from this year Old Trafford has acknowledged the cricketing battles of the rival roses really began. For several years at this period the side was predominantly amateur with the Rowleys and the Hornbys always prominent. Professionalism was not scorned. Almost every match saw the employment of one or two paid players, and of the very early Lancashire professionals none were more persistent than Reynolds and Iddison, although it falls to the credit of one William Hickton to gain distinction as the first Red Rose bowler to capture all ten wickets in one innings. He did so in 1870 when he dismissed every Hampshire batsman at a total cost of forty-six runs in their second innings at Old Trafford in a match that brought him figures of 14-73; in 1867 at Lord's he had picked up eleven Middlesex wickets for ninety-one runs, only to be on the losing side. Hickton, like many of Lancashire's cricketing 'professors' of those days, was not born in the county. He came from Derbyshire and was good enough to play for the Players against the Gentlemen at the Oval in a career stretching from 1842 until 1900.

If Iddison and Hickton set the pace as the men to star with bat and ball, there were amateurs playing alongside them who could also contribute more than their fair share to a three-day game of cricket. A. N. Hornby, in point of fact, topped the county batting averages from 1869 to 1872 although he had to yield to a parson the distinction of being the first amateur to score a century for Lancashire in championship cricket; in 1869 the

Reverend Frank Wynward Wright scored an unbeaten 120 against Sussex and was also commended for his brave fielding, 'close up at point'. Wright was not Lancashire born; he came from Oxfordshire but was educated at Rossall School where his mighty deeds on the cricket field are still compared to those of A. G. Steel and R. H. Spooner who followed Wright into both the Rossall and the Lancashire sides, and brought ability and style to bear in tremendously impressive careers. Wright, unlike Steel and Spooner, was never able to spare the time for regular first-class cricket. He settled down to a scholastic job in Eastbourne and was really lost to the game before his rare gifts had time to mature.

Once the 1860s had given way to the new names and more comprehensive fixture lists of the 1870s Lancashire gained both in cricketing strength and reputation; foremost among the men who mattered with bat and ball at this still transitional period in first-class cricket were two professionals, Alec Watson and R. G. Barlow. At once Lancashire became a harder side to beat and in 1872, with Watson and Barlow in fine form, the four matches against Yorkshire and Derbyshire were all won impressively. Barlow, it is recorded, took a wicket with the first ball he ever bowled in top-class cricket (against Yorkshire at Sheffield) and he was always, in a career spanning the years 1871-91, thirsting for more. A career record of 726 wickets at 13.59 per victim suggests he was seldom disappointed and it is a fact that in Lancashire's triumphant double victories over Yorkshire and Derbyshire in 1872 all the bowling was done by Barlow, Watson and one William McIntyre. Between them they captured seventy-three of the eighty wickets that fell, and the other seven were all run out! One wonders what the amateurs in the side thought about this well-nigh unprecedented piece of cricketing piracy?

It was the same trio of bowlers who enabled Lancashire to face up to the change that came into the first-class game in 1873 when rules and regulations were drawn up to control the qualification of players and put a stop to the profitable meanderings of the leading professionals. All three were given verbal promises of security under the new deal, and with the ageing but still useful Fred Reynolds seconded to coaching duties with a special mission to arrange and sustain the strength of the teams which Manchester fielded in club matches in between county engagements, the pattern of Lancashire cricket took on a shape that endured until the advent of the first world war and even afterwards. The names were different but the pattern was the same, and it stood Lancashire in good stead.

Powerful on the field and well administered off it, there could be no question but that Lancashire played a full part in the cricketing scheme of things to be as the nineteenth century drew to a close; perhaps the only blot on their record from the administrative point of view came when they refused to support the introduction of a cup competition into the first-class game. The suggestion came from Lord's but Lancashire, who had representatives on all important committees, considered that 'with first-class cricket becoming more popular every year there was no need for the new idea'. It was later disclosed that when the topic was debated in the Old Trafford committee room there was a general fear that cup cricket would encourage gambling on the game and such a thing could not be risked. It is to Lancashire's credit that many years later they were bold and brave enough to change their mind and support the inauguration of the Gillette Cup with determination and enthusiasm. Lord's ' lost the toss '. Lancashire's attitude was endorsed by a majority of the other county clubs and cup cricket was taboo. There were other matters demanding attention. Increased interest brought bigger crowds to watch the game and Lancashire had to give thought to improvements at Old Trafford, both for their members and the general public. A bigger pavilion was planned and more seating provided for the masses on the popular side. And with this new surge of public interest came the need to encourage the best players to make their way to Old Trafford.

The all-powerful Lancashire League, or the Central Lancashire League which covered wide areas of the county then regarded as 'distant' from Old Trafford, offered no competition – that was to come – and several players of the highest class, amateur and professional began to appear in the county side. Vernon Royle, Richard Pilling and A. G. Steel first appeared in 1877; a little later Johnny Briggs, Johnny Crossland and George Nash, professionals with character as well as ability, also brought their many gifts to the first-class cricket scene. Qualification rules were not all that irksome to Lancashire at this period, although in their first match under the new regulations Yorkshire came to Old Trafford and won in two days, to raise some doubts. When a second defeat was sustained at Sheffield later in the year still more eyebrows were raised and questions asked about Lancashire's ability to be self-supporting from the cricketing point of view. Surrey, however, were well and truly beaten twice that year when 'Monkey' Hornby hit the first of his many centuries for the county and Watson and McIntyre outshone the out of touch Barlow in the bowling line. Edmund Rowley skippered the side, doing so with distinction and tact, but major honours eluded a team frequently chopped and changed around to accommodate amateur players when they were available.

The first breakthrough was made in 1879 when Lancashire shared the county championship with Nottinghamshire with a record of five victories, four draws and one defeat in a ten-match programme. Success was welcome but a joint share was not considered enough. In 1881, under the captaincy of A. N. Hornby, Lancashire gained the championship, going through a thirteen-match campaign unbeaten, with ten victories and three draws emphasising the balance and the strength of a side that Hornby had welded into a tremendous cricketing force. The captain topped the batting honours list, averaging fifty runs an innings, hitting three centuries, and also claiming the season's highest score with a superb 188 against Derbyshire. And this was the time of W. G. Grace! Hornby enjoyed splendid batting support from A. G. Steel, Watson, Robinson and Barlow, and with the ball, Barlow, Nash, Steel and Watson were the men who mattered. The campaign began on a high note when Derbyshire were thrashed at Old Trafford where they were dismissed for 102 and then saw Hornby and Barlow pass that total in an opening partnership of 157 with 118 of the runs credited to the captain. The victory set the tempo, and wherever they played Lancashire were in great form.

The club took a rest from championship cricket in mid-season to play Cambridge University in a match to mark the opening of the Liverpool club's new ground at Aigburth; it was generally conceded that the university side of 1881 was one of the strongest ever. They had the three Studd brothers, G. B., J. E. K. and C. T., to start their innings and coming later were three Lancashire players, A. G. Steel, O. P. Lancashire and J. R. Napier; on a difficult pitch the university triumphed, the only team to beat Lancashire that summer. Defeat in a friendly encounter did not affect Hornby and his men in championship matches and the only two counties to avoid defeat were Nottinghamshire, Surrey and Gloucestershire, and at Clifton it was the weather, not the powerful influence of the immortal W. G. Grace, that saved the west country side from defeat.

A year later Lancashire again shared the title with Nottinghamshire, losing one match out of sixteen, winning twelve and drawing three; the prime feature of a still successful season was the improvement shown by Crossland who claimed ninety-seven wickets for ten runs each. Alas, Crossland's success did not go unquestioned. Opponents and spectators alike did not relish the fast bowler's action and although no umpire ever called him to order and no definite rules and regulations were in being to decide between a fair and unfair delivery there were times when Lancashire's delight in victory was tempered by criticism of the manner in which it was achieved.

Somerset and Kent were by now welcome additions to the Lancashire fixture list, but the highlight of the summer in many eyes was the clash against Gloucestershire at Clifton when four of the best batsmen in the country, Hornby and Barlow for Lancashire, vied with W. G. and E. M. Grace in the opposition ranks. All four played attractive innings and Lancashire scraped home by thirteen runs. A visit to the Oval saw the first real demonstration against Crossland and his suspect action. Although the Lancashire bowler claimed eleven wickets in the match, his performance 'gathered as much abuse as praise from a partisan Surrey crowd'. Lancashire's victory was duly recorded, but in the club's records there is mention of some dissatisfaction at the manner in which it was achieved. Today, with mass newspaper coverage and the spotlight of television, such a game would have aroused world-wide attention. Neither Hornby, as captain, nor the club, officially accepted that Crossland's action was unfair, and by the time the season ended the incident of the match was regarded as closed. It was not!

3. TROUBLED DAYS

In peak form throughout the 1881-2 seasons, Lancashire slumped the following summer, losing five of the twelve games played and winning only six in spite of a successful start to the campaign and against Oxford University, when Robinson (154) and Taylor (96) put together a fourth wicket partnership of 237 to create a record that stood until twelve years later when A. C. MacLaren and A. Paul hit up their memorable 424 against Somerset at Taunton. Again Crossland bowled well but came under fire. The Oval partisans again proved the most difficult and it is on record that an angry scene in the pavilion between innings, embracing players and followers of both sides, delayed the continuation of the game for half an hour and an abandonment was narrowly averted. Twice Yorkshire defeated Lancashire to make the slump even more hard to bear, and in the match at Sheffield a crowd of ten thousand saw Ulyett do the hat-trick and hit up sixty-one runs in a dashing manner. The seasonal averages indicated a loss in batting power, with Hornby far less consistent and Steel unable to play in half the programme, but by far the worst repercussion of a drab season came when Nottinghamshire refused to accept fixtures against Lancashire because they harboured 'grave doubts about the fairness of the bowling of two players'. Crossland obviously was one and it was generally conceded that Nash and Watson, although slow bowlers, also lacked the smoothness of action generally desired. Lord Harris, of Kent, was another who openly objected to Crossland and refused to have the Lancashire bowler in his England team.

Lancashire, to their credit, backed up their players in the absence of complaints from the umpires, but there was more trouble in the offing when the qualifications of several players were questioned, Notts leading the way with a statement insisting that ' the only rules necessary for players in the side are that they shall either have been born in or resident in Lancashire '. In view of such feeling it caused no surprise when, in 1884, Lancashire won only seven of their twelve championship matches and lost four of them. Crossland kept his place in the side in spite of the winter allegations and took seventy-two wickets for thirteen runs each in an attack in which both Watson and Barlow claimed over a hundred wickets each. Lancashire's weakness was certainly not in the bowling line and a disappointing season was marred still further when the county's game with Gloucestershire was abandoned because of the death of the mother of W. G. and E. M. Grace.

The 1885 season was another troublesome one for Lancashire, and the Crossland controversy came to a head when, after Kent had been beaten at Old Trafford, Lord Harris, the Kent skipper, wrote a long letter to the Lancashire committee outlining his objections to Crossland's action and recalling that the Old Trafford officials had declined to follow the lead of other counties in agreeing not to employ bowlers with doubtful actions. Stressing that he had no fault to find with A. N. Hornby's conduct or captaincy, Lord Harris declared that although the umpires had not no-balled either Crossland or Nash, it was his firm opinion that both threw, and he would ask Kent to allow the return fixture at Tonbridge to go by default. Lancashire made a vigorous reply, defending their bowlers and boldly sending copies of the correspondence to Lord's, pointing out that the MCC had chosen Crossland to play in the annual North v South match at headquarters, thus implying their satisfaction with his action! The quarrel raged on for some weeks but ended curiously with Crossland allegedly breaking his qualification by residing for several months in Nottinghamshire. The MCC committee banned the controversial fast bowler and he played his last game for Lancashire against Cheshire in a non-championship fixture at Stockport in June 1885. He was much missed but Johnny Briggs made rapid strides as a left-handed spinner, and taking seventy-nine wickets for ten runs each admirably filled the gap caused by Crossland's enforced retirement from first-class cricket. Two records were set up that summer; G. M. Kemp hit the first

Lancashire century against Yorkshire in an admirable 109 at Huddersfield, and Briggs (186) and Pilling (61) put together 173 runs in a hundred minutes for the last wicket against Surrey at Aigburth. No Lancashire last-wicket pair has ever done better and the record still stands today. Despite the disappearance of Crossland from the side, Kent acceded to Lord Harris's request not to entertain Lancashire at Tonbridge and so ended another turbulent season for Hornby and his men.

With Crossland gone, news of Lancashire's need for a new fast bowler spread far and wide. It produced one remarkable character in Bennett Hudson, a Yorkshireman with a vast experience of professional cricket in the leagues that were then springing up in the north of England. Hudson qualified for Lancashire by means of engagements with the Bacup and Longsight clubs and in 1866 he made an impressive début – as a batsman! Played for his bowling, Hudson had the effrontery to hit a remarkable ninety-five against Sussex, followed by eighty-five at Oxford, and his effort against Sussex was a furious affair containing sixteen boundary hits and so exciting his captain and his colleagues that he was awarded a county cap on the spot, the coveted head gear being hurled to him through the pavilion window by a captain who allowed his gratitude of the moment to overrule his discretion.

Given a trial as a pace bowler, Hudson played in only five matches and took but three wickets before he went back to the leagues with a reputation as a capped player for a county that managed to win more matches than it lost, but still found championship honours out of reach, despite a joint honour with Nottinghamshire and Surrey nine years earlier, until 1898. That was the year in which two more prominent names began to find distinguished mention in Lancashire cricketing circles. Albert Ward and Arthur Mold came along, and with Arthur Paul also establishing himself the side, still led by the irrepressible A. N. Hornby, began to take on a challenging look once again. Ward, like so many of Lancashire's cricketing immortals, had played for Yorkshire before he came to Old Trafford and his first season, in 1889, brought him an impressive batting record of 822 runs for an average of thirty on the kind of pitches that gave bowlers far more satisfaction than batsmen. A double win over Yorkshire made the season – just as it would today – and but for vital defeats against Middlesex, Nottinghamshire and Gloucestershire a third share of the championship honours might well have been bettered.

The 1890 season brought further disappointment. Lancashire finished second to Surrey, winning only half of their fourteen championship games and losing three, and this was the year when illness robbed the county of a vital figure in the side. Wicket-keeper Pilling never recovered from a serious winter illness, and despite a convalescent voyage to Australia was unable to resume his brilliant career. His absence had a marked effect on the fielding of the side and as Briggs missed a month's cricket through injury and Barlow lost his bowling form the summer passed with Hornby and his men earning marks and points more for tenacity than impressive cricket. Yet this was a year never to be forgotten as the years wore on. A. C. MacLaren made his début and with a chanceless 108 hit in 130 minutes against Sussex at Brighton, gave due notice of magnificent things to come. His display held out promise of batsmanship of irreproachable style and masterly dignity. The new boy, straight from Harrow, succeeded after the side's more experienced batsmen had failed, and this was the beginning of an era aptly described as the golden one in Lancashire's cricketing history.

In 1891 Lancashire again finished runners-up to Surrey with a record of eight wins, three draws, four defeats and one abandonment in championship cricket. They suffered because illness limited the appearances and performances of the redoubtable Briggs and recurring strains reduced Watson's bowling prowess. In addition, and this was probably of greater importance, the new boy MacLaren could play in only five matches. He did not reach the century that summer but still topped the batting averages to provide further evidence of a majestic career ahead. The season ended with the official retirement of Barlow and the partial one of Hornby as captain, and these two events brought to an end a chapter with many bright pages and summers of much delight. There had been times of stress, occasions of controversy. There were also moments of sheer cricketing delight and although there was sadness all around at the going of Barlow and the desire of Hornby to take a back seat there were those behind the scenes at Old Trafford who forecast that the best was yet to come.

Unfortunately, MacLaren was not yet available regularly, and an appeal was made to Hornby to continue in charge of a team ready for the rebuilding. A man with eleven glorious years of faultless leadership behind him could not refuse to do the game he loved or the county he so richly adorned a further favour. He undertook the joint captaincy along with S. M. Crosfield for two or more seasons, stepped off the field to do yeoman work in committee, proudly took over as club president in 1894 and then, in another emergency, returned to the field and the captaincy in 1897-8. It was a remarkable achievement by a remarkable man, and although stern in appearance and spartan in outlook, Hornby not only commanded attention but won tremendous respect from all who played with or against him. And, strange to relate, he was never once heard to object to his nickname of ' Monkey '. In his later years Hornby always insisted his career officially ended with the closing of the 1891 season, but his efforts for Lancashire remained consistently invaluable until well into the twentieth century and he actually held the presidency from 1894 until 1916. The men he handled were remarkable and reliable. He controlled the Crossland throwing controversy with diplomacy, insisting upon his beliefs but never losing friends because of them. He supported the maligned fast bowler against all charges and never once gave a temperamental player cause for complaint. Even in the leisurely days towards the end of the nineteenth century temperament and tantrums were not unknown on the cricket fields of England.

In the main, good sound captaincy and shrewd discipline hid the unsavoury features from the public gaze, but Lancashire, like all counties, had their moments when players stepped out of place. That they were quickly admonished and restored to sanity was a tribute not only to Hornby's flair for leadership but also to his understanding of men, especially those who earned their living in what was then still predominantly an amateur sport. When his first term ended, at Hornby's own request, Lancashire were in a quandary. The young MacLaren had neither the time nor the experience to step in and Crosfield was brought in to share the burden with Hornby who played only four matches in 1892 and again only four more in 1893 – and they were erratic years in the history of the club, albeit in 1893 the side finished runners-up to Yorkshire in the championship. The title was in the balance until the closing weeks of the season, when Lancashire lost three vital matches and Yorkshire won three. Disappointing though the outcome was, there was consolation. It was in 1893 that one John Thomas Tyldesley made his début for Lancashire. Alongside Archie MacLaren he was destined to usher in the club's undisputed 'golden era'.

4. MACLAREN STEPS UP

Sporting history is full of stories about men who win fame. Some earned it the hard way, others had it thrust upon them. In a sense, that was the way it was with MacLaren but no man ever rose to the occasion with greater flair or effect. Lancashire invited Crosfield to continue as captain in 1894 and a likeable cricketer accepted. Unfortunately he was unable to fulfil his obligations and just before the campaign opened he asked to be excused. It was the year when A. N. Hornby assumed the presidency rôle and, although there is nothing to indicate so, it can be taken for granted that the 'old man' was not only in favour of MacLaren stepping up but also promised him full support. What is more, he kept his word – and that did not always happen, as Lancashire found to their cost much later on. At twenty-two MacLaren was without doubt the youngest captain in the country and the one with least experience, and when his side started off with a series of disappointing results there were some, remote from Old Trafford let it be said, who were critical of a youngster being asked to do the sort of job that called for experience not only of cricket but also of men. Nonetheless MacLaren rode the storm. His leading batsmen struggled to find form, and his principal bowlers, Mold and Briggs, toiled willingly on. In the end seven championship matches were won, seven lost, one drawn and

another tied. When the final reckoning was made, Mold had taken
144 wickets and Briggs 97, but there were no really outstanding
batsmen. Even MacLaren, topping the averages as if by divine
right, had played with no outstanding distinction although a press
cutting of the day revealed that 'the young MacLaren appeared
to gain in leadership stature match by match and it was noticeable that his professionals acknowledged and sustained him at all
times'.

J. T. Tyldesley did not figure in Lancashire's plans that
summer, after a brief sight of him the year before, but in 1895
John Thomas really arrived to open his career alongside a captain
who had spent the winter in Australia and missed his county's
opening fixtures. MacLaren soon made up for lost time. He
played the innings that still ranks as the 'highest ever' in the
cricketing history not only of Lancashire but of all England. It
was Somerset who felt the power and the majesty of MacLaren
at his very best. At Taunton he made a truly magnificent 424 out
of a Lancashire total of 801, batted in all some 470 minutes, hitting sixty-two fours and shared with Ward (64) an opening partnership of 141 followed by one of 363 with Paul, whose contribution of 177 was in itself a superb innings, though completely
overshadowed by the record-breaking of MacLaren who left the
previous best of 344 by W. G. Grace well behind as he carved
his place in cricket legend. Eventually dismissed with the total
792 MacLaren emerged as a truly great batsman. His Taunton
efforts did not exhaust him. In a season that saw his side play
twenty-two championship games to win fourteen, lose four, draw
one and see another abandoned, the captain finished the summer
with three successive centuries on pitches far from batting
paradises. MacLaren, of course, headed the averages, both for
county and country. Ward, Paul and the newcomer, Tyldesley,
also played well.

Tyldesley made the first of his many centuries with a fine innings of 152 against Warwickshire very early in the season, and
the Manchester sporting public showed their appreciation of the
cricket played under MacLaren by going down to Old Trafford
in their thousands. The Kent match drew twenty thousand on the
first day and when Yorkshire crossed the Pennines in August, a

crowd officially returned at 25,331 went through the turnstiles to enjoy the sort of cricket only the rival roses representatives can provide. At the final reckoning Lancashire were again next best to the champions, Surrey, and in 1896 MacLaren, limiting his appearances to ten matches but scoring 713 runs, saw his team's record bettered only by their deadly Yorkshire rivals. To make up for MacLaren's irregular appearances, Sugg, Baker and Ward, along with the still maturing Tyldesley, all batted well, and it was Sugg who contributed the most notable innings of the summer with a splendid 220 scored at a run-a-minute rate against Gloucestershire and W. G. Grace at Bristol.

The season opened with some off-the-field battling as Lancashire, pleading with Yorkshire to establish bank holiday meetings at Whitsun and August as seasonal fixtures, considered the White Rose reply lacking in grace and courtesy. So heated were the exchanges that Lancashire made the correspondence available to the *Manchester Guardian* and the *Sporting Chronicle*, and until the breach was healed Kent were prevailed upon to come to Old Trafford each August bank holiday – an arrangement that continued for several years until better relations were established across the Pennine Range. Finishing as runners-up in five seasons out of seven, Lancashire planned to go one better in 1897, and with MacLaren expressing a wish to be relieved of the leadership, A. N. Hornby, then fifty years of age, was persuaded to return; that season the title was won outright with sixteen matches won, seven drawn and three lost.

The prime features of a successful campaign were the captaincy of Hornby, the batting of MacLaren, Tyldesley, Ward, Baker and Sugg, and the emergence of a new bowler, Willis Cuttell, who, like so many before him, was Yorkshire-born but available to Lancashire because of a professional engagement establishing residence at Nelson. Cuttell began his first-class cricket career at the age of thirty-two and captured 102 wickets in his first season. With Briggs back to his best form, picking up 140 victims, and Mold (88) and Hallam (90) in support, Lancashire's attack was undoubtedly the most varied and successful in the country. With the bat, MacLaren, almost casually, averaged over fifty an innings, and Ward and Baker contributed their quota by each topping the thousand run mark. Tyldesley and Sugg were not far behind and Lancashire lacked nothing in the field with a new wicket keeper, one Lees Radcliffe, who stepped in for the injured and often brilliant Smith, evoking memories of the immortal Pilling in his neatness and style against fast and slow bowlers alike. The following year brought disappointment at the overall results, with only nine matches won, six lost and eleven drawn and the championship passing to Yorkshire in a summer bedevilled by much rain. In spite of adverse conditions Cuttell became the first Lancashire player to do the double of a hundred wickets and a thousand runs. MacLaren played only occasionally after a strenuous Australian tour which also left Briggs stale and out of touch; with Mold handicapped by a knee injury, on the whole it was a season of hard work and little reward for Lancashire.

One man, however, emerged successfully from the damp, slow and often difficult pitches that abounded. J. T. Tyldesley hit 1,918 runs with an outstanding double century against Derbyshire, confirming all the good things said about not only his ability but his temperament. The little man had come good, and in 1899 he continued to display the sort of batsmanship that established him among the élite of the cricketing world.

The last season of the nineteenth century saw Lancashire facing difficulties on and off the field. Hornby was pleased to be allowed to settle down to final retirement; MacLaren had to think about a business career and could not promise to make himself available with any degree of regularity – a factor that had caused him to miss much cricket in the two previous years. It was agreed that MacLaren should take over the captaincy jointly with G. R. Bardwell, but neither could play regularly and finally Hornby answered the call once again. When Briggs, preferred to Rhodes for a test against Australia, broke down with illness and was admitted to a mental home, Lancashire's problems mounted in spite of further progress by the dapper Tyldesley and the advent of another talented batsman in Jack Sharp. As always, however, the shutting of some doors was accompanied by the opening of others and with the century drawing peacefully to its close another Lancashire batsman destined to make a name for himself appeared on the scene.

His name was Reginald Spooner and he had distinguished himself at Marlborough School and began his career with Lancashire by hitting a delighful century for the second team against Yorkshire on a Middlesborough pitch far from idea for the purpose. Spooner was invited to make his championship début against Middlesex at Lord's and although on the losing side the young amateur made his mark by hitting forty-seven and eighty-three in impeccable style. In a season of no real impact, perhaps the highlight was the clash between Lancashire and the Australian tourists at Old Trafford, a match dominated by Trumper and Tyldesley. Trumper made eighty-two but Tyldesley followed with two terrier-like innings of fifty-six out of a total of 102 and a second innings of forty-two out of eighty-one.

And so the century turned. Lancashire cricket was well established. Great deeds by batsmen and bowlers alike had been coupled with shrewd and often memorable captaincy. Difficulties had been encountered and overcome. Tantrums had been displayed and dispelled. Professionalism had been encouraged and wisely controlled. Behind the scenes Old Trafford had been secured and improved. Public support had been wooed successfully. Finance presented no real problems. Money was available when required but none could be recklessly squandered. Administration had been on an honorary and a devoted basis. Men who were not good enough to play, willingly gave their time and energy to keep the books, make the decisions, and generally ensure Lancashire were as strong and efficient off the field as they were on. They also serve who work behind the scenes! When the twentieth century dawned, the pitch had been well and truly prepared. Lancashire was ready for any cricketing challenge.

5. FIRST INNINGS

If it can be rightly assumed that the first fifty years are the most critical, it must never be overlooked that as time goes on, building on solid foundations also presents problems; but at the beginning of the twentieth century there can be no denying that Lancashire entered upon their golden era. It could not be otherwise with the majestic Archie MacLaren as captain and such talented cricketers as Reggie Spooner, Johnny Tyldesley, Walter Brearley and the master bowler Sydney Barnes in the team. Yet in terms of championship successes the early years of the new century were far from distinguished ones. MacLaren led the side from 1900 until 1907 but it is recorded that only in 1904 were Lancashire county champions. It is true MacLaren and his men were always placed in the first four in the memorable years in which he led not only Lancashire but England and the Gentlemen of England and was at his mightiest best. His brand of batsmanship was never in question. His ability to master the best bowlers had been proved time and time again. He continued to score consistently and with flair. So did the batsmen under his command. His bowlers, too, met every challenge with determination and no little skill and if there was only one championship to rejoice in during MacLaren's eight years of undisturbed leadership there could be no questioning the character and the style with which Lancashire endowed their cricket. And it must not be overlooked that this was the era in which Neville Cardus first devoted his attention to the game and his beloved county. No club ever had a better chronicler of events. It can be said that the prose of Cardus matched the brilliance of Lancashire's cricket, and without doubt this delightful writer played no little part in building up the legend that was Lancashire cricket in the period bedevilled by two world wars.

Cardus has said, many, many times, that it was MacLaren who lit the spark under his literary furnace. He worshipped him as the complete cricketer and few would care to dispute any of the many glorious tributes Cardus paid to a man who meant to Lancashire what W. G. Grace meant to Gloucestershire and England, what Lord Hawke epitomized in Yorkshire cricket and, a generation later, what Sir Pelham Warner did for England and Middlesex. MacLaren walked tall in the best of company. He could never be overlooked and seldom failed to fill either a field or a room with his commanding presence. One man can never make a team, yet MacLaren did his best to make Lancashire cricket the envy of all other counties in the early years of the twentieth century. In the 1900 season MacLaren and his men won fifteen out of twenty-eight championship fixtures, drew eleven and lost only two encounters. Although Spooner was absent on military duty in Ireland, Briggs made a brief recovery from a distressing illness and so, too, did Hallam. Along with Briggs and the tireless Mold there was Sharp and also Webb to make up a testing bowling array and among the batsmen there appeared the stylish C. R. Hartley and H. G. Garnett, amateurs of the MacLaren mould and run scorers to revive nostalgic memories, even if Yorkshire did steal the honours by going through the campaign unbeaten. Lancashire's record was good enough to win the championship nine years out of ten, with Tyldesley and Ward lending their captain major batting support and Briggs highlighting the season by taking all ten Worcestershire first innings wickets at Old Trafford.

The season, alas, was not without its unsavoury incident; Mold, who took ninety-seven wickets in support of the centuries gained by Briggs and Cuttell, was no-balled for throwing at Nottingham, and as Sydney Pardon thundered in *Wisden* that Mold's playing days are nearly over, the county captains met to confirm the sad fact. Mold tried to cure his fault but was called again in the early days of the 1901 season when Lancashire won eleven games out of twenty-eight, drew twelve and lost five. They failed to disturb Yorkshire at the top of the table and Mold was one of the casualties. Briggs and Cuttell were others. Briggs' recovery in 1900 was followed by a recurrence of illness and he had to go. Cuttell broke a bone in his bowling hand and almost at a swoop Lancashire lost three top-class bowlers, for all had played for England. Sharp and Webb strove mightily to heal the breach. Each claimed more than a hundred wickets but it took brilliant batting to keep Lancashire within sight of the championship for most of the year. In all matches the dapper little Tyldesley topped three thousand runs and Garnett developed into a very useful ally. MacLaren, of course, continued to bat as only he could and took it upon himself to start the hunt for new bowlers. His search led him to the Lancashire League, then enjoying, along with the Central Lancashire League, a boom period for crowds who could neither afford the money nor spare the time to support

The Lancashire team in 1879 (joint champions with Nottinghamshire). *From left to right, standing,* Rowbotham, Nash, Pilling, MacLaren (James), Watson, Barlow; *seated,* Crossland, Haigh, Hornby (A. N.), Taylor; *front row,* Robinson, Royle (V. K.), Briggs

below
The Lancashire team in 1890; the captain, A. N. Hornby, wearing a blazer, is in the centre of the second row

Lancashire in 1894. *Back row, left to right*, Mold, Paul, Lunt (scorer), Baker, Smith (A.), Sugg; *middle*, Ward, Tindall, MacLaren (captain), Bardswell; *front*, Briggs, Smith (C.), Tinsley

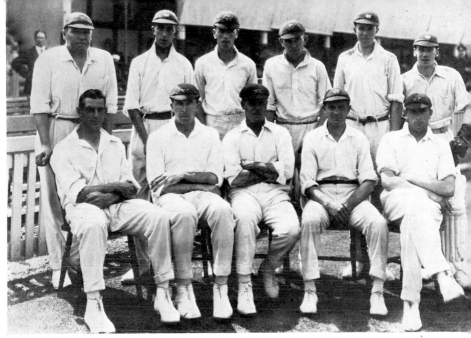

Lancashire in 1925. *Back row, left to right*, Dick Tyldesley, Jack Iddon, Len Hopwood, Frank Watson, Frank Sibbles, Bill Farrimond; *front*, Ted McDonald, J. R. Barnes, J. Sharp, Harry Makepeace, Cec Parkin

below

Lancashire in 1933. *Back row, left to right*, Eddie Paynter Will Horrocks, Len Hopwood, Frank Booth, Albert Bennett, Frank Sibbles, Len Parkinson; *front*, Frank Watson, Jack Iddon, Peter Eckersley, Ernest Tyldesley, George Duckworth

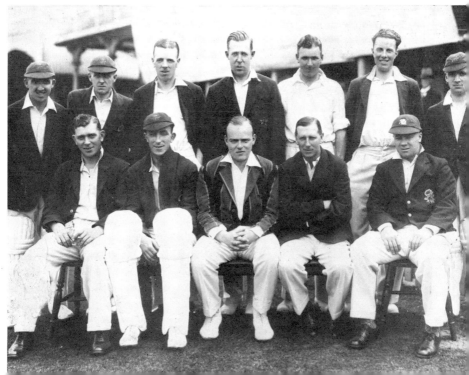

Above, four famous
Lancashire players of the
1880s, *left to right*,
Richard Pilling, Alec
Watson, A. N. Hornby
and R. G. Barlow

George Duckworth,
probably the 'prince' of
all Lancashire wicket
keepers

the county team at Old Trafford. Barnes, tall, gaunt and dourly blessed with a temperament that demanded that he give of his best at all times, had ignored previous pleas to try his luck with Lancashire. He recognised the magnificence of MacLaren but thought little of the terms offered him to leave the leagues and concentrate on the first-class game.

It is one of the legends of Lancashire cricket that MacLaren had never seen Barnes bowl in a match when he decided to take him to Australia. What he had seen was Barnes at the nets. What is more, he had batted against this tall, unsmiling attacker and satisfied himself that he possessed the skill and determination to master Australian batsmen on their own near-perfect pitches. MacLaren deplored the attitude of the Lancashire committee in their dealing with Barnes but did not let it lessen his regard for a master bowler. He took him to Australia, saw him succeed, and brought him back in the mood to play first-class cricket with Lancashire. In point of fact the winter of 1901-2 was a controversial one for Lancashire. At the end of the previous summer MacLaren, disappointed with results and dissatisfied with the committee's handling of other affairs, announced his desire to relinquish the captaincy. It was accepted. The great man took his England team off to Australia in something of a huff and did not stay to congratulate Alex Eccles on his appointment to succeed him in the Lancashire captaincy. He even hinted at a desire to go and live in the south of England for the benefit of his wife's health, but all ended well. MacLaren returned from Australia without the ashes but with Barnes establishing not only as a good bowler but a great one. In a remarkable change of mind MacLaren decided to continue with Lancashire and considered that with Barnes to pinpoint his attack the county championship was again within reach. He was doomed to disappointment. Barnes was never quite the bowler on English pitches that he was in Australia and his first season's haul of eighty-two wickets was well below expectations. In the summer of 1902 Lancashire won only seven championship matches, drew eleven, lost five and suffered one abandonment; Yorkshire remained champions.

Barnes was a cricketing enigma. He looked the best bowler of his kind and proved it in Australia where MacLaren nursed him carefully and shrewdly placated him in his moments of depression. It was easy on tour but in the hurly-burly of county cricket, with twenty-four championship matches to play, Barnes found the going hard. He was never a popular man among his fellow professionals. Perhaps he was too much of a perfectionist. It was not in his nature to bowl anything but flat out and when he saw colleagues merely going through the motions on unsympathetic pitches he rebelled. MacLaren had to ask a lot of him and although the gaunt Barnes never once complained and would do anything for his captain, inwardly he was ill at ease. He pined for a return to league cricket where he was lord of all he surveyed and where he could stipulate his own terms, financially and on the field of play. In league cricket, Barnes was more than a club professional. He was the captain, and almost the team itself. He took the wickets and seldom left his batsmen much to do. In this environment he took great delight and his contribution to the first-class scene with Lancashire was a limited one – some forty-six matches, bringing him 225 wickets. It is fair to assume that if MacLaren had not been captain at the time, Barnes would never have bothered to play for the county or for his country – a tragic waste of the best possible cricketing talent. Unhappy in 1902, Barnes was still out of his element in 1903 and even the advent of Walter Brearley as his new ball partner and the regular appearances of Spooner to strengthen and burnish the batting could not shake the mighty Barnes out of his depression.

He bowled well. His pride would not allow him to do otherwise, but Lancashire were never in touch with the leaders, losing five matches against ten wins and eleven draws, and seeing Middlesex take over from Yorkshire at the head of affairs. There were, of course, stirring events, with Barnes and Brearley sharing all twenty Surrey wickets at Old Trafford and MacLaren and Spooner delighting with an opening partnership of 368 against Gloucestershire at Liverpool, even if, as some reports suggested, 'neither batsmen was quite at his best'. The critics were hard to please in those days! In 1904 Lancashire lost Barnes but Hallows did the 'double' and Brearley was in tremendous form. With MacLaren, Tyldesley and Spooner batting superbly, the side went through the season unbeaten, winning sixteen matches and drawing the other ten. Lancashire were champions again, with Yorkshire a poor second and Kent an even worse third.

MacLaren was contented. He regretted the departure of Barnes but accepted the inevitable. An unhappy bowler was an indifferent one from Lancashire's point of view, and so Barnes returned to the league where he built up a legend and maintained it until he reached his sixties. Lancashire's success in 1904 earned them a game against the rest of England at the Oval, and a memorable match saw both MacLaren and Jessop at their best with Spooner and Tyldesley playing other significant roles. When the statistics of the season came to be finally reckoned, Lancashire had won the title in magnificent manner, scoring their runs at never less than eighty per hour and occasionally topping the hundred. It was undoubtedly their golden age.

But even in their hour of triumph Lancashire had problems. Brearley, surprisingly omitted from MacLaren's side that met the Rest of England, threatened retirement and coupled his threat with the intention of going into the leagues who were then drawing crowds of five thousand at times, and splitting the cricketing public of the county in two from the allegiance point of view. The workers settled for league cricket. It was played on Saturday afternoons when they were free, and, what is more, little was demanded from the travelling point of view. As one old-time cotton worker put it: 'Tha's got to be a man o'means to watch first-class cricket . . . and besides tha's expected to wear a collar and tie when tha goes to Old Trafford.' Indeed you were, and the privileged members sported tall hats and frock coats as they took their place on the pavilion side.

In 1905 the Australians were touring England and Lancashire had much to contribute to the England team of the day. MacLaren, Spooner, Tyldesley and the eventually pacified Brearley who was persuaded to stay with the county were all in demand for the test matches. Lancashire, unlike Yorkshire, could not withstand such losses and still win county matches. They were successful in twelve of their championship encounters, drew ten more, lost three and saw one game abandoned and the title went once again to Yorkshire. Yet in the early stages of the summer, MacLaren and his men gave no hint of collapse. But once the test matches came along it was soon apparent the reserves at Old Trafford could not cope with the situation. Cuttell's skill deserted him and Hallows could not recapture his form with either bat or ball. Poidevin was introduced, and began to exploit his googly with some degree of success although, of course, this then new-fangled kind of spin lacked accuracy and was often expensive. Nonetheless Poidevin proved himself a thoroughbred of a cricketer by hitting five centuries and topping the batting averages. Runs were not the problem. Twice the side topped the six hundred mark and in one memorable encounter with Nottinghamshire at Trent Bridge Lancashire totalled 627 against a side that employed eleven bowlers – yes, even the wicket keeper had a go! Spooner hit a century before lunch and Tyldesley hit a magnificent 250 in a chanceless innings spread over five hours.

Three weeks later Sussex were hit to the tune of 601-8 and this time it was Hallows who did the damage with a whirlwind 130 runs in 110 minutes. A few days later Somerset saw their total of 401 topped in less than four hours with only four wickets lost. Such was the power of the batting at MacLaren's command. His bowlers were unreliable, although in one enchanting day's cricket against Somerset at Old Trafford, Brearley touched the heights by claiming nine wickets for forty-seven runs in dismissing the opposition for sixty-five before lunch. By close of play Lancashire had answered with 424-8 with 139 of the runs coming in the last forty minutes cricket. To further burnish this fantastic Lancashire victory Brearley went on to take four wickets in four balls and capture seventeen wickets in the match.

Things were not quite the same when Gloucestershire visited Old Trafford and Brearley and Jessop fought out a tremendous cricketing duel. The major honours went to Jessop, and in the closing stages it was reported that 'tempers became frayed and Brearley resorted to the bowling of full tosses, many of them head high'. The batsman won the battle. In four overs Jessop and Board hammered Brearley for fifty-seven runs but the fast bowler eventually dismissed the pair of them and Lancashire snatched a victory, soured by the manner in which it was achieved. Jessop took exception to the tactics and even went to the length of criticising Brearley in print and threatening never to appear at

Old Trafford again. Cricket was not without its sensations even in those leisurely days. The championship was lost but Lancashire were still a match for the best.

It was the same in 1906 when Brearley and MacLaren began to show signs of the wear and tear of some hectic cricketing seasons. Brearley played in only five matches and MacLaren missed more than he played. The upshot was that six championship matches were lost, against fifteen won and five drawn and the championship went to Kent. Cuttell showed a welcome return to form in what proved to be his last full season, and although the side's top batsmen continued to score their runs attractively, consistency was lacking, although the ever-watchful Tyldesley and the stylish Spooner enjoyed moments of great delight and Heap often came along with some telling batsmanship up and down the innings. Dean, a left-hand spinner, made his first appearance and Huddleston, on the verge of regular selection for several seasons, finally made a place of his own. For the first time the name of Makepeace appeared on the teamsheet and 1906 saw another prominent cricketer make his début at Old Trafford. His name was Woolley and he was to sustain Kent and England for many years to come.

6. THE END OF MACLAREN

By 1907 MacLaren had begun to feel the strain. He retained the leadership and lost none of his enthusiasm. Yet he found runs harder to score and days in the field were a trial to a man in his middle thirties. Brearley could not play with any degree of regularity, Cuttell had gone to coach at Rugby School, and Findlay had left to take the administrative side of the game with Surrey.

In a word, Lancashire had to rebuild. It proved to be a season of close finishes and one not without incident. Heavy rain ruined the county's match against Middlesex at Lord's and, whilst the captains debated whether to continue after a long inspection of the pitch, a section of the crowd invaded the middle to size things up for themselves. MacLaren objected strongly, and after assessing the damage refused to allow his side to continue. He issued a statement to the press to justify his action and was supported by the groundsman who asserted repairs to the pitch were beyond his capabilities. The argument raged for days but the imperious MacLaren would never yield from his original and irrevocable decision not to carry on even if evidence was forthcoming that, once he and his team had departed, the heavy roller ironed out all traces of the damage done by the invading crowd. Dean asserted himself with a hundred wickets in his second season and Huddleston worked hard. So did the two Cook brothers, Billy and Lol, but there was nothing better throughout a difficult season than the batting of the dapper Tyldesley on pitches that were often difficult and at times treacherous. Sharp rendered yeoman service in support and although MacLaren played a few memorable innings he and Hornby dominated a match against Derbyshire at Chesterfield with an opening partnership of 162 in 105 minutes, Dean followed up with an outstanding return of 9-46.

The season ended at Blackpool and MacLaren's days as Lancashire's captain were over. He was destined to play again and to captain England yet again, but the old mastery, the majestic presence and the imperious attitude were seldom in evidence in MacLaren's later years. A. H. Hornby took over the captaincy in 1908 and retained it until the outbreak of the first world war. His leadership was impressive and his batting of great value but it was his lot to follow MacLaren and no man could hope to earn comparison. It was said of the new captain that he loved hunting more than cricket but there could be no denying his determination to succeed. His batsmanship was tinged with daring and his fielding was fearless and tireless. His attitude to the professionals in the side started on a brusque note but he learned to appreciate their problems and even fight their battles. He took over when new bowlers were badly needed and in his first season only ten championship matches were won against nine lost, six drawn and one abandoned.

Brearley, now a cricketer of moods but still a fast bowler to be feared, reappeared and did his best to give Hornby the attacking spearhead so essential. Brearley's success was measured by 148 wickets at fifteen runs each and even if Old Trafford's pitches were well below standard this was a remarkable effort by a bowler with a past rather than a future. The faithful Dean plodded skilfully on at the other end to Brearley and his left-handed spin brought him 124 wickets, but Lancashire were never really versatile or deadly enough in the field to threaten Yorkshire, who regained the county championship. As ever, Tyldesley was the side's main batsman and his 243 at Leicester was the season's highest score. Sharp lent admirable assistance but Spooner played only once and when MacLaren did turn out he never really got going; a very ordinary season ended with Old Trafford coming under the critical eye of a groundsman from the Oval, sent north to examine and report on the complaints received from visiting counties about the state of the pitches provided. An inspector of pitches was apparently nothing new even in the early days of the century!

Forced to occupy a middle-of-the-table place, Lancashire were far from happy, and a tremendous effort was made in 1909 to get back among the leaders. Alas, Hornby simply did not have the ammunition. His side lacked nothing in courage, but of the twenty-four championship matches played, fourteen were won, four lost and six drawn; with no real challenge to Kent they emerged champions again. For once, Tyldesley was far from in top form, but there was compensation. His younger brother, Ernest, made his first appearance and the name still meant much to Lancashire cricket although the newcomer was destined to have a lengthy wait for full recognition. Amazingly, Brearley retained form and fitness to capture 115 wickets, with useful assistance from the tireless Dean, Sharp and Lol Cook, whilst Heap enjoyed more success than usual, but now it was the turn of the batsmen to lose consistency. Makepeace made rapid strides to aggregate some nine hundred runs but MacLaren could not recapture form and, with the elder Tyldesley for once lagging behind, there was never enough stability to enable Hornby and his men to provide more than ordinary resistance to the better equipped counties. There were, of course, notable victories as well as defeats. Twice Surrey were beaten handsomely, with Sharp hitting a fine century and Brearley and Dean bowling superbly at the Oval, injuries to Hobbs and J. N. Crawford, coupled with bad luck, with the weather denying Surrey their revenge at Old Trafford.

Dean had two remarkable match returns. Against Warwickshire at Liverpool he took nine first innings wickets for thirty-five runs when Hornby put the opposition in. In the second innings the left-hander followed up with 4-46 and Huddleston had 6-19 to justify fully their skipper's boldness on winning the toss. This was the match that first saw the younger Tyldesley, Ernest, introduced and an innings of sixty-one hinted at the shape of delightful things to come. Perhaps the best batting came at Worcester, where J. T. Tyldesley and Sharp hit 237 in 150 minutes, and at Eastbourne where Spooner and Hartley took 208 for the first wicket against a by no means impotent Sussex attack.

In the winter of 1909-10 Lancashire went to Lord's and persuaded the other counties to simplify the points system in the championship, hitherto based on a percentage tally. Retaining a percentage in the final column, Lancashire proposed that victory be the deciding factor in determining the title; neither for the first time nor the last the Red Rose county was to lead the way in administrative matters. They believed that the new system would encourage more positive cricket but it availed Hornby and his men little. They won fourteen of their twenty-nine championship fixtures, drew ten and lost five, once again providing little threat to the leaders although finishing fourth to Kent, Surrey and Middlesex. The major reason was an injury to the mercurial Brearley, who played in but three games and left the attack without a penetrative spearhead. The faithful Dean nobly did his best to capture 133 wickets with his economical and often deadly spin but the pace of the dynamic Brearley was sadly missed although Huddleston, Heap, Whitehead and Cook all had their moments of success. Fortunately, J. T. Tyldesley recaptured his form to score more runs than any other batsman that summer and top the first-class averages with half a dozen centuries to his credit.

7. HISTORY IS MADE

The season saw Lancashire's batsmen make history. For the first time in championship cricket a side hit more than four hundred runs to win a match. It happened against Nottinghamshire at Old Trafford, and for two days Lancashire were outplayed. Hardstaff hit a century to enable his side to reach 376 in the first innings and all the home team could do in reply was reach a modest 162 against the skilled and varied attack of Wass, Clifton and Iremonger. A. O. Jones, the Nottinghamshire captain, refused to enforce a follow-on and sent his batsmen out again to ensure victory with slow-motion tactics that recoiled upon them on the last morning and left Lancashire to hit exactly four hundred for victory in five and a quarter hours. In stepped elder Tyldesley to put on 191 of the runs in 150 minutes and then came the other Tyldesley and Whitehead to add a further eighty in forty minutes before a minor collapse occurred. What followed was more in keeping with the stories told in boys' magazines, but it is true that Lancashire had resigned themselves to defeat because their captain A. H. Hornby was suffering from cartilage trouble and limping badly. Hearing of this, a member with some medical knowledge but no professional qualifications hastened from the bar to the dressing room with a request to be allowed to 'work' on the damaged leg. Hornby was desperate. Out there in the middle Lancashire were up against it. Some eighty runs were needed in an hour and the injured captain was the sole remaining batsman. To cut a long story short, John Allison, the member in question, successfully 'treated' Hornby and he went on to hammer out a magnificent fifty-five not out to win the match and be carried from the field shoulder-high. And what is more, the 'cure', whilst not permanent and certainly not ethical, enabled Hornby to finish out the season which then had six weeks to run.

These last six weeks were distinguished by victories over Yorkshire and Hampshire and by an occasional appearance by MacLaren with a touch of his old arrogance and mastery who took

D

one look at a rough Birmingham wicket and then thrashed the Warwickshire attack for a century in eighty minutes. That was MacLaren at his imperious best.

Once again, in 1911, Lancashire finished fourth in the championship table. They were still led by Hornby and won fifteen, drew eight and lost seven of their thirty matches in a season that comprised one of the busiest on record. It was also a summer of sheer delight from the batsmanship point of view. The elegant Spooner, available for three months, reached his peak with 2,300 runs and an average of fifty-six, and nowhere did they feel the impact more than at the Oval where the handsome amateur hit 224 out of his side's 360, with Sharp's thirty-five the next best innings. Brearley was on the wane. Playing in only ten games, he was inconsistent and expensive, but Dean toiled nobly on to claim 183 wickets and top the country's averages. Lol Cook, like Dean an unfashionable but tireless bowler, stepped in to render most support with eighty-five victims but with Spooner in such majestic flow it was the batsmen who made the news in 1911. Johnny Tyldesley was then approaching forty but he was never easy to dismiss and averaged forty for his county as did the reliable if self-effacing Sharp, a cricketer of such all-round prowess and always doing something useful. Makepeace and Ernest Tyldesley, two of the younger batsmen, contributed modestly but promisingly in a campaign waged on brilliant batting lines to win back the crowd support so strangely diminishing the previous summer. But, then, who could resist Spooner at his best!

County cricket took a back seat in 1912. A triangular tournament between England, Australia and South Africa dominated the summer and cut most counties down to a championship programme of some twenty-two matches. Lancashire won eight of these, drew ten, lost two and saw two abandoned in a season of soft and often difficult pitches. Dean and Huddleston made the most of the conditions and Dean at long last gained test match recognition. Despite the poor quality of the pitches, Ernest Tyldesley made the first of his many centuries in 1912 and although his elder brother saw his test career more or less ended he remained on hand to score more runs than anybody else for his beloved Lancashire.

Who could doubt which match provided the best cricket? When Surrey came to Old Trafford, first Spooner and then Hobbs made centuries – and never was batsmanship of higher or more memorable vintage, for grandfathers, fathers, grandsons and even great grandsons have been told of the great deeds of that match dominated by two batsmen who 'moved in elegant manner their wonders to perform'. Yet even the good things of the summer were for a time forgotten in the closing days of the season when the temperamental Brearley announced the day had come when he could no longer bowl his fastest and his fiercest, and therefore he had no intention of carrying on. And so passed from the scene a fast bowler of moods but also one of many great gifts. Never again were Lancashire members and supporters to see him leap the fence that divided the pavilion from the field at Old Trafford. Gates were made for ordinary cricketers. Brearley had little use for them!

By the time the 1913 season began, Lancashire were in sore straits. Brearley had gone. Spooner had injured himself severely in the hunting field and cricket was out of the question. In addition Hornby lost his touch with the toss. It is a good captain who can combine great playing gifts with leadership qualities and also bless his luck with the coin. Hornby had done well in all branches but in 1913 his skill and his luck deserted him and both were contributory factors in a season that saw more defeats than victories. In cold print, eleven games were lost, seven won and eight drawn, and Lancashire were no more than an ordinary side. The two Tyldesleys, Makepeace and Hornby managed to gather in enough runs to present a respectable front and Heap, Huddleston, Dean and Whitehead saw to it that opposing batsmen did not have things too easy. But there were no outstanding figures, albeit Johnny and Ernest Tyldesley did enliven the summer with one glorious week in which both hit centuries at Leicester and then went on to the Oval where the elder batsman hit 210 and Ernest 110. Even in adversity Lancashire had their moments.

The bad patch continued throughout 1914 with only half a dozen victories to record against nine defeats and eleven draws. Dean broke down with an injured knee, and then got at loggerheads with the club committee, and the bowling was sadly lacking both in guile and striking power although one new man appeared and brought a touch of character to the scene. His name was Cecil Parkin, and like Sydney Barnes he came reluctantly to Old Trafford from the Lancashire League where he had brightened up the scene with Church and successfully hidden the fact that he was Durham-born. In 1914 Parkin briefly hinted at genius and sensation. Before he could make his mark, war broke out and cricket was forgotten. But before the dark days dawned Johnny Tyldesley had again shown remarkable versatility and endurance to top the averages and play a notable innings against Hampshire at Liverpool when he hit 122 not out in a total of 228 shortly after hitting a masterly 253 at Canterbury.

The Hampshire match was also a good one for Dean, who took thirteen wickets and the season was also noticeable for the appearance of another Hallows – Charlie was the nephew of William and was to become a stylish adornment to Lancashire cricket once the first world war had been fought and won. It began just before the season finished and Surrey were declared champions as players everywhere exchanged their white flannels for khaki uniforms and Old Trafford's history-steeped pavilion was turned into a hospital for some eighty sick and wounded servicemen. Apart from Johnny Tyldesley, who was too old for active service, Lancashire sent an entire team to battlefields all over Europe and for those who stayed at home there was the task of keeping a club alive, without cricket, for four long and weary years in which battles were more important than bats and guns counted for more than wickets.

8. FAITHFUL MEMBERS

Throughout the first world war Lancashire's members remained remarkably faithful and some seventeen hundred continued to pay their subscriptions for the duration of the enforced stoppage. Their money enabled Lancashire to survive and do a little bit to ease the wartime problems with donations and kit for prisoners of war, and, at the same time, fulfil their obligations to the players on the staff. The war years were endured and by 1918, with an end of hostilities in sight, Lancashire called their committee together again to discuss a resumption of first-class cricket. Surprisingly, there was a gloomy atmosphere prevailing and the county decided to support a plan for two-day games as a 'feeler' to the way back. The experiment was tried in 1919 but survived only that season, although much of the cricket was good enough to watch and by no means deficient in the skilled arts. Inevitably every county had players who had paid the supreme penalty on the battlefield and in the Old Trafford pavilion they unveiled a tablet honouring Lancashire's dead. A new era demanded a new approach. Lancashire had to consider the terms upon which their old players could be attracted back to the game and they succeeded in meeting financial demands with a fixed scale of £5 a match, and £1 expenses at home and £3 away. In addition there was inaugurated a winning bonus system of £1 a man and the captaincy was entrusted to M. N. Kenyon, a player of modest ability but a leader of men and a figure to be respected by all and sundry. Although J. T. Tyldesley's best playing days were behind him when play reopened in 1919 the grand old-timer returned to Old Trafford to try again at the age of forty-six. Lol Cook and Parkin were not immediately available but Lancashire ushered in a new cricketing decade with eight victories, twelve draws and four defeats in 1919. Four years of inactivity had left an inevitable query against Dean's ability to maintain length, spin and direction and the left-hander's return of 51 wickets at 30 runs each clearly indicated his best days were over. When Cook was finally demobilised he at once added power to Kenyon's attack and with the advent of another Tyldesley, who took 71 wickets, a fair showing was made.

The new bowler, James, was no relation to the batting Tyldesleys. He came from the productive Bolton area and was to be followed by a younger brother, Richard, a spinner who was to bring both skill and character to Lancashire cricket a little later on. A new era brought younger names to the top. Ernest Tyldesley led the batsmen with Makepeace close behind and in third position was the graceful Hallows, second only to Yorkshire's Sutcliffe in the new brigade of English batsmen to be. Johnny Tyldesley did his best to keep pace with his younger colleagues, but in spite of one glorious fling of 170 against Gloucestershire at Old Trafford when he hit seven sixes and seventeen fours the old-timer found the going tough. Spooner did not reappear until almost the end of the season, when he took over the captaincy for a match or two, but he found form hard to regain. The championship went to Yorkshire but Lancashire had few complaints. They had felt their way carefully and were confident that they had the material with which to rebuild a side capable of competing with the best.

It was a belief well founded. In 1920 Lancashire made a great effort to get to the top of the championship table. They won nineteen of their twenty-eight matches, drew four and were beaten five times before yielding top spot to Middlesex in a dramatic climax to a season of much good cricket. So close was the finish that Lancashire, beating Worcestershire early on the third day in the final match of the season at Old Trafford and noting Middlesex were in trouble against Surrey at Lord's, began to celebrate a little too soon. Jack Sharp, leading the team in the absence of Kenyon, wisely pleaded for moderation until success was beyond argument, and he was proved right. Middlesex recovered, took the title, and made some Lancashire players and members feel a little sheepish. Despite the disappointment there was satisfaction behind the scenes. Not only had Lancashire played good cricket; they had also introduced the new men so necessary to repair the ravages of war. Johnny Tyldesley had to give way, proudly and with all honour. His brother took over, and along with Makepeace and Hallows he became the cornerstone for the next few years as far as batting was concerned. Spooner, like Johnny Tyldesley, had to admit his best days were behind him but new young amateurs like J. R. Barnes, F. W. Musson, G. O. Shelmerdine and A. W. Pewtress made their appearance, and with Kenyon's health breaking down, Sharp took command. Bowling problems were solved when Parkin successfully returned, wooed from Rochdale in the Central Lancashire League as an occasional player, and Dick Tyldesley got to work with his artful spin and plaintive appeals. Lol Cook remained the stock bowler but Dean was on the wane after years of devoted and honourable service.

Middlesex retained the championship in 1921 and Lancashire slumped to fifth place despite the powerful batting of Makepeace, Hallows and Ernest Tyldesley, and the success of Cook and Dick Tyldesley with the ball. Perhaps it was the glorious weather of the summer that saw Lancashire fail. Certainly the hard and fast pitches that abounded helped the side's main batsmen to enjoy themselves but they forced the bowlers to labour long and wearily for success. Kenyon, back in harness and in charge, saw the gallant Cook toil manfully on to claim 143 wickets but Parkin was still only an occasional player and Dean was getting less and less effective as his career came to a close. The amateurs Shelmerdine and Barnes made notable contributions and a new young professional in Frank Watson gave promise of consistent batsmanship in the offing. And 1921 was, too, the year when Dick Tyldesley first demonstrated that his vast girth – he weighed some seventeen stones – was no barrier to deadly fielding close to the wicket. He picked up six catches in one innings against Hampshire, the same match in which Parkin stressed how valuable a man he could be by taking fourteen wickets in the match at a cost of 180 runs – an analysis not to be equalled by many ' spare-time' bowlers and one that caused the Lancashire committee to open negotiations with Parkin and the Rochdale club in an effort to secure a talented bowler in a full-time capacity. If further proof was needed of Parkin's value it came at the Oval when, without the Rochdale professional, 1,004 runs were scored and only twenty batsmen were dismissed. In the words of the impartial reporter, 'both sides lacked sparkle in attack!'

By 1922 Lancashire had secured Parkin on terms that guaranteed his regular appearances and there were high hopes that his ability to bowl fast with the new ball and spin or cut the old one would enable the county to clinch the championship. But it was not so. Lancashire was undoubtedly a stronger side but so, too, were several of the other counties and Yorkshire began a run of four successive title wins, with their ancient rivals yet again filling the number five spot. What went wrong? Parkin proved his value by capturing 172 wickets, and with Cook and Dick Tyldesley as steady as ever the attack proved as good as most others even if Dean had finally gone. Yet again Ernest Tyldesley,

Makepeace and Hallows dominated the batting, but only fifteen matches were won against seven lost and eight drawn. Parkin had several remarkable matches, taking eleven wickets against Glamorgan and another eleven against Worcestershire. He followed up with a first innings analysis of 8-47 at Gloucester and another match haul of 14-73 against Derbyshire at Chesterfield, but there were times when a highly talented but temperamental bowler was freely punished and his side could not clinch victories that appeared within their grasp. It was irritating – but it was cricket.

At the end of the campaign Myles Kenyon resigned the captaincy and Jack Sharp took over. For years this dapper Merseysider had done sound work with bat and ball. Like Makepeace, he was an all-round sportsman. Each gained international honours at soccer and cricket and it is Lancashire's proud boast that few if any other county had ever fielded two 'double' internationals in the same side. Be that as it may, in 1923 the new captain ran into an immediate problem. James Tyldesley withdrew from the side and Cook began to show signs of the wear and tear he had cheerfully shouldered for several seasons. It left Parkin and Dick Tyldesley to carry a tremendous burden. Both were primarily spinners and the kind of bowlers who do their best work when the fast bowlers have made a breach with the new ball. Although fifteen out of thirty championship matches were won against thirteen drawn and only two defeats, Lancashire were never serious challengers for the title then securely in Yorkshire's grip. Sharp suffered through illness and for the Yorkshire match a harassed committee recalled Johnny Tyldesley to skipper the side at the age of fifty. As usual, Ernest Tyldesley, Makepeace and Hallows answered most batting demands and for the first time Makepeace topped the two thousand run mark, playing a memorable innings of 106 out of 208 against Nottinghamshire at Trent Bridge and following on with double centuries against Worcestershire and Northamptonshire. Hallows missed several games through illness but scored fluently and consistently when fit. He made up a formidable trio of Lancashire batsmen but it was in attack, where, despite the brilliance of Parkin and Dick Tyldesley, Lancashire lacked depth.

Parkin could not be faulted. He took 176 wickets in championship cricket and 209 in all first-class games and had no complaints to make when Dick Tyldesley 'seconded' his efforts by topping the hundred wicket mark. One good pace bowler was the missing link and tremendous efforts were being made to find the man who could do the job. Again Lancashire turned to the leagues, and the man they eventually signed was E. A. McDonald who had been the scourge of the England batsmen alongside the fiery J. M. Gregory when the Australians had been riding roughshod over our cricket grounds in 1921. McDonald was signed from Nelson in time to brighten up Lancashire's diamond jubilee year in 1924 and long before the season began the betting men were laying the odds on McDonald making Lancashire into an unbeatable team. He almost obliged. The team, still captained by Sharp, went until mid-August before going down to a defeat against Glamorgan and ending the campaign with another defeat against Kent in a summer which saw eleven matches won, two lost and seventeen drawn. It was the seventeen draws that prevented Lancashire from ousting Yorkshire as champions and finishing up in fourth position after batting against the odds of formidable opposition and the kind of weather that make cricket a nightmare. Of a dozen matches at Old Trafford only two were played to a finish and wherever the side went the rain followed them. With McDonald eager to impress he got nothing but mud heaps to bowl upon. Yet, alongside Parkin and Dick Tyldesley, he made up a tremendous trio and 366 batsmen fell prey to them in the course of championship cricket.

Parkin himself revelled in the weather-affected pitches. He took over two hundred wickets but talked himself out of the England team with an unwise and unpardonable attack upon his country's captain. Few sides built big totals against Lancashire in 1924 and perhaps the greatest degree of satisfaction in a disappointing campaign came when Yorkshire were defeated, dismissed for a mere thirty-three at Leeds where Dick Tyldesley and Parkin were the conspirators in chief. In the annals of all the mighty cricketing battles between Lancashire and Yorkshire none have quite upset the odds as this one did and mention is made elsewhere of a tremendous bowling achievement. The batsmen, naturally, took second place in this rain-ruined summer but the work of Ernest Tyldesley, Makepeace and Hallows left no room for complaint. They were effective on bad pitches as well as good ones and that, surely, is the hallmark of class.

9. DUCKWORTH ARRIVES

Bad luck with the weather ruined Lancashire's hopes in 1924 and the following summer, when nineteen championship matches were won against nine drawn and four lost, it was misfortune of another kind that prevented the side from achieving their championship ambitions. Sharp, still the appointed captain, suffered much from injury and illness but the greater and more vital blow was the loss of Ernest Tyldesley half-way through the season after he had averaged over fifty runs and produced the sort of form that linked him with his elder brother as one of Lancashire's batting immortals.

As always, however, adversity in one direction presented opportunity in another. Watson, for several years an improving batsman, really came into his own, and behind the wicket there appeared the talented and perky Duckworth. Sibbles was another newcomer and it was generally agreed that Lancashire, with an attack comprising McDonald, Parkin, Dick Tyldesley and Sibbles, was as strong as any in the county championship. In the all too frequent absence of Sharp, Barnes or Pewtress took command and it was perhaps the handicap of no settled captain or policy that prevented the side from breaking Yorkshire's stranglehold on the championship. In spite of a sequence of slow and unresponsive pitches, McDonald bowled beautifully to capture 182 wickets in championship cricket and pass the two hundred milestone in all matches. His pace and the movement of the ball through the air and off the pitch were devastating but it was the tall and dark Australian's action that compelled attention and evoked admiration. He ran up silently and moved into action with such grace and rhythm that he became the embodiment of all that was best in bowling. His arm action was as high as any purist could wish for and his wrist cocked like a deadly cobra ready to strike. In addition his body action could not be faulted. Not too much chest and just enough shoulder swing. McDonald looked and was the perfect bowler. He was also a man of moods and a difficult cricketer to placate when things were not going right. In the mood he was masterly. Out of it he often drove captains and comrades to despair.

McDonald owed much to the agile and lively young Duckworth behind the wickets. A recruit from the Warrington area Duckworth lacked inches but was never aware of it. He had a voice that never faltered and his shrill appeals would liven many a dull cricketing moment. He was superb standing back to the pace of McDonald and adept at coming close up to take the spin of Dick Tyldesley and help lure batsmen to their doom by nimble stumpings and extraordinary catches. In cooperation with the often playful Parkin, Duckworth contributed much to Lancashire's pleasing cricket in 1925. He played his part, too, in helping Sibbles to top the bowling averages. The newcomer's return was a modest forty-three victims at thirteen runs each. He was employed when the three terrors, McDonald, Parkin and Tyldesley, were out of touch or out of action and he seized his chance admirably, mixing his movement through the air at a brisk medium pace with an ability to turn or cut the ball from the off. With Makepeace, Hallows and Watson covering up as best they could for the missing Tyldesley, who had undergone an operation for appendicitis, Lancashire not only proved attractive players of the game but good crowd pleasers, and Old Trafford frequently housed more than ten thousand spectators at weekends with six thousand or so attending during the week.

They were good days, and they foreshadowed an era of terrific success. But unfortunately Sharp contributed little. Far from fit, he tended to bulkiness and was suspect in the field. His crowning error was to drop a simple catch off Parkin at the start of the temperamental bowler's benefit match against Middlesex. H. W. Lee was the batsman to escape first ball and Sharp's blunder not only precipitated a big opening partnership but roused the big crowd to sarcastic comment and unmerciful barracking. Sharp was upset and at the end of the season he resigned the captaincy and retired from a game he had served nobly and well.

Lancashire debated the question of their captaincy long and often throughout the winter that separated the 1925 and 1926 seasons. In the end they chose wisely and few men rose to the occasion in the manner of Leonard Green. A fine club batsman and a man with an outstanding military record, Green, a major in the army during the war, stepped up to command a Lancashire side full of talented individuals. Men like McDonald, Tyldesley, Parkin and Duckworth were masters of their cricketing craft but, as so often happens, when talent borders on genius temperament appears. It says much for Major Green that he took over and at once installed discipline and commanded respect. He was a stern man but a fair one. He lacked MacLaren's flair as a player but treated his men with more understanding. Each and every one of them grew to admire the new skipper and worked devotedly for him to end a spell of no championship success from 1904 until, in 1926, they ousted Yorkshire from the top of the table and went on to record a hat-trick of wins that remains the high spot and the most successful period in Lancashire's long cricketing history. Under Green, in his first year, Lancashire won seventeen championship battles, drew thirteen more and were beaten only twice, and when all was over Yorkshire, who had not been beaten, reluctantly handed over the championship pennant.

A memorable season was not without its incidents. The temperamental Parkin bowled well in between off spells and in order to impress a master bowler with the necessity for concentration and endeavour the new captain took the unprecedented step of dropping him. Parkin took offence and immediately announced his intention of returning to league cricket. It was a sad ending to a brief but highly profitable interlude in the cricket of the county but Major Green was adamant. The good of the game and the welfare of a side rapidly growing in strength and prestige could not be sacrificed by the whims of any one man. Parkin went and Iddon stepped in. Again, misfortune for one player presented opportunity for another, and Lancashire sealed the championship with a magnificent closing victory over Nottinghamshire at Old Trafford.

Ernest Tyldesley was not only Lancashire's batsman of the

year but also the run scorer of the summer. In one glorious period he produced a spell of ten innings in which he topped the half-century mark in every match to score 1,477 runs and return figures only Don Bradman has ever equalled. The summer of 1926 was certainly Tyldesley's high noon and with Neville Cardus to record his masterly achievements Lancashire lacked nothing in skill and determination on the field and masterly appreciation off it. The championship years of 1926-7-8 were also tremendous years for Cardus. In the two Tyldesleys, McDonald, Parkin and Duckworth, he had cricketers extraordinary to write about. There was also the dour Makepeace, the stylish Hallows and the defiant Watson to provide further material. In Lancashire alone Cardus created legends about each and every player, and the opposition were never ignored. Yorkshire were also blessed with men like Robinson, Sutcliffe, Holmes and Macauley, to say nothing of the ageing Rhodes and the rotund Kilner. Between the two counties Cardus was in his seventh heaven. His prose matched the artistry and the dignity of the players who moved in front of him. They were truly great cricketing days!

Green led the Lancashire side with great diplomacy. His discipline came to be accepted as essential and his handling of the men under his command was masterly. They were allowed their fling but answered to the captain for any indiscretion. Rebukes were administered behind the closed doors and complaints were similarly dealt with by a captain who defended his men in committee and on the field. It was leadership of the highest order and Leonard Green was undoubtedly one of Lancashire's most successful leaders. His record proves it. But it really needed no embellishment. The players respected their skipper and gave him all they could in the way of effort, skill and loyalty. In a nutshell, the major welded rich talent and wayward genius into disciplined teamsmanship. Each and every man had a part to play, and each did so to the best of his ability. No captain, or club, could ask for more, and Lancashire were champions in every respect.

10. NEVER FOUND WANTING

It may be argued that Green's batting was far from outstanding, but the captain was never found wanting in a crisis and his qualities as a leader more than atoned for his modest run-scoring returns. As Duckworth once so perkily reminded all and sundry on one joyful occasion: 'Skipper's aw reet. He does his job and we do ours.' It was the same in 1927 as in 1926, despite a lot of bad weather and seventeen drawn games. Ten championship matches were won and only one lost. Again Makepeace, Hallows, Tyldesley and Watson were the run scorers and McDonald, Dick Tyldesley and Sibbles shared the wickets. Watson and Iddon made notable contributions in all-round capacities and Duckworth was at his zenith as a wicketkeeper beyond peer. There were charges of slow scoring levelled during the season but the weather and the state of the pitch was mainly responsible. Makepeace, of course, was always classed as a stone waller, and Watson was tarred with the same brush. Yet both could attack if and when the need arose. What is more important, each earned a reputation as a good bad wicket player, and every championship side needs such fighters.

The captain neither condoned nor condemned slow scoring. He often instructed Makepeace and Watson to lay a solid foundation and encouraged his later batsmen to build on it. He aimed at four hundred runs a day as a minimum and few today would complain on that score. He supported a Makepeace declaration that to show respect to bowlers before lunch was no sign of weakness but merely a necessary prelude to a successful onslaught afterwards. And Lancashire often made the period between tea and close of play a batting paradise. There were times when visiting batsmen meted out similar treatment, and it was in 1926 that a young man came north with Gloucestershire and played an historic innings against McDonald. His name was Hammond and he tuned in at Old Trafford with a magnificent 187, hit in three hours of exquisite batsmanship. It speaks much for Leonard

Green's sense of fair play that he led the applause as the young newcomer returned to the pavilion. At the height of their achievements Lancashire were never averse to paying tribute to the opposition.

When the balance sheet was drawn up at the end of the 1927 season it was noticed that Hallows, Makepeace and Ernest Tyldesley had not been the prolific scorers of the previous summer. Each had contributed well over a thousand runs, but nevertheless they had not dominated the scene quite so much. Similarly, McDonald and Dick Tyldesley had topped the hundred wicket mark and yet not been the masters of old. Lancashire's margin over Nottinghamshire at the top of the table was in percentage terms 68.75 against 67.85 and the critical ones at Old Trafford were holding forth about complacency in the ranks. Green disliked this attitude but could do nothing about it, except to impress upon his team that in 1928 he wanted them to answer back.

They did so nobly. Of the thirty championship matches played, fifteen were won and fifteen drawn. Defeat was avoided and Hallows made the first attack upon the critical members and followers by hitting a thousand runs in May and doing so with such style and dignity that even the more vehement of the complainers were silenced. It was a summer of brilliant weather and perfect pitches. Batsmen everywhere were in clover and Lancashire looked no further than the old brigade of Hallows, Makepeace and Ernest Tyldesley for the bulk of their runs. Iddon and Watson contributed steadily and steadfastly and Hopwood earned mention with all-round performances of promise. From the weather point of view 1927 was akin to an Australian summer and McDonald, although then in his mid-thirties, enjoyed himself immensely. Given pace in the pitch the old magic returned. He played in every championship match and took 178 wickets at nineteen runs each to delight the crowds, impress the opposition, and stir Cardus to new heights of lyrical prose.

As ever, Dick Tyldesley was McDonald's main assistant, but for once the burly spinner failed to reach the hundred wicket landmark. He finished with eighty-five victims at thirty-one runs each and began to complain that batsmen ' weren't playing back as often as they should '. Tyldesley's bluff was beginning to fail

but it was years later before Wilfred Rhodes was heard to proclaim that 'Dick only thowt he turned t'ball', following that up
with a friendly word of advice to always play forward to him and
runs would come. Be that as it may, Lancashire still ranked
Tyldesley highly, and with Watson, Iddon and Hopwood getting
wickets in any emergency a hat-trick of championships was completed. It was noticed, when the final figures were examined and
the books audited, that Makepeace's power was on the wane. The
old-timer with the broken nose had eventually stepped down from
the number one position in order that the younger Watson could
gain experience in a key position. The skipper was alive to the
needs of the morrow as well as the requirements of the hour! So
well did his plans work out that Watson and Hallows, joining up
as it were in mid-season, contributed twelve three-figure partnerships, while Hopwood was back after a spell in league cricket to
contribute 566 runs and thirty-three wickets in twenty games.
Duckworth showed no signs of wear and tear. The little Warrington wicket keeper dismissed 107 batsmen and by his verve
and personality did much to enliven the Lancashire cricketing
scene.

By way of celebration the team went to Blackpool to play Wales
in a friendly encounter and nearly came to grief against a veteran
bowler; Syd Barnes captured six wickets in his fifty-sixth year
and had not Hallows hit a dignified century the champions might
well have been beaten. As it transpired they were defeated in the
very last match of a glorious summer. Lancashire took on the
might of the rest of England at the Oval and were beaten by an
innings and ninety-one runs with Larwood, Tate and Freeman
getting the wickets and Hammond dominating the batting. During the winter Major Green reluctantly announced that he could
not continue to play first-class cricket because of business
demands. The question of his successor needed much thought,
for the departure of the captain at a time when the side's batsmen, Ernest Tyldesley and Makepeace, were getting to the
veteran stage and the two main bowlers, McDonald and Tyldesley,
were also getting older presented a major problem. In addition,
a section of the club members made it plain they were none too
keen on 'outside' help. In essence they appreciated what the likes

64

of McDonald had done but they wished to see native-born talent given more encouragement.

To meet their wishes Makepeace succeeded J. T. Tyldesley as coach and Sydney Barnes was recalled to help find and train young bowlers. Eventually P. T. Eckersley was appointed captain. He was never more than an ordinary player but he was a good leader of men and had the time to spare. In following Leonard Green, however, he undertook a tremendous task and in 1929 Lancashire lost their championship title to Nottinghamshire, winning only twelve of their twenty-eight championship battles and drawing thirteen, with three defeats also recorded. Lord's in their wisdom introduced larger wickets that season and insisted upon each county playing the same number of championship fixtures with points taking over from percentages as the governing factor in deciding the outcome of championship competition. As usual, Ernest Tyldesley remained the bulwark of the side's batting but Hallows fell from grace and although Watson was as consistent and successful as ever Makepeace was recalled late in the season to stiffen the batting. The old-timer duly obliged. He topped the averages but virtually ended his career by a tremendous effort calling for the sort of physical demands a man of forty-seven could not easily provide, especially after a sporting career all the year round as a first-class soccer player as well as a cricketer. Old Harry did his best and a mighty good best it was. He was one of Lancashire's most faithful servants and he stayed on at Old Trafford in a coaching capacity for many more years to come.

McDonald took 140 wickets in spite of a natural slowing down and Dick Tyldesley came back to form with 136 victims, but the next best bowler could muster no more than forty-four wickets and the season was more noticeable for what opponents did rather than for what Lancashire achieved under Eckersley. None the less the new captain was well liked and commanded respect. So much so, in point of fact, that in 1930 he led the side to the championship once again. What is more, Eckersley had the satisfaction of leading an unbeaten team with ten matches won and eighteen drawn. Once again the weather was far from ideal for cricket, but there was no decrying the splendid form of the team's 'old men'. Ernest Tyldesley averaged fifty-nine runs an innings and never

E

missed a match. McDonald and Dick Tyldesley again dismissed over a hundred batsmen each and the Australian did not hide his delight when he bowled Bradman at Liverpool just as the touring side were beginning to build up a legend of invincibility. Hopwood with sixty-three wickets, and Sibbles with forty-nine, made notable contributions, and Duckworth was as good as ever behind the stumps, but it was the batting Tyldesley, then in his forty-fourth year, who earned the accolade as Lancashire got back on top. Warwickshire felt the strain of Lancashire's power when McDonald shattered them with a hat-trick at Birmingham and Tyldesley hit his best-ever innings of 256 not out in the return match at Old Trafford.

It was late in the summer before a new name appeared on the Lancashire team sheet. Eddie Paynter made his début and another glorious era of batsmanship was born. With Eckersley now established as a successful captain, Lancashire had to win three of their last five matches to withstand a Yorkshire challenge with Dick Tyldesley bowling his heart out ambitions were fulfilled and celebrations in order. Alas, success was short-lived and in 1931 only seven games were won against seventeen drawn and four defeats. Inevitably the demise could be traced to the inability of McDonald to sustain both form and fitness. He had bowled superbly for six seasons and that was a long time for any fast bowler to retain form and fitness. Instead of over a hundred wickets McDonald took only twenty-six and played in fourteen matches before announcing a desire to retire and return to the comparative ease of league cricket once again. In addition, Watson had a painful and prolonged illness and Lancashire were suspect in both batting and bowling. Dick Tyldesley remained as consistent as ever with 116 victims, and Sibbles increased in form and stature by dismissing eighty-two batsmen at moderate cost. Yet, in the very first match of the campaign, Sussex hinted at the shape of things to come when Tate bowled the southern side to a well earned victory and the reaction was obvious when Eckersley took his men to Worcester and saw them beaten for the first time in that county. Perks and Root were the bowlers who did the damage and Lancashire never recovered from their bad start. Kent and Freeman rubbed salt in the wound and there was nothing of outstanding merit to save the side from a very ordinary season in which few reputations were enhanced. It was the same in 1932 when Dick Tyldesley lost an argument with the committee over his wage demands and hied himself back into league cricket while still capable of top-class bowling. Eckersley was left to struggle on as best he could with Ernest Tyldesley his senior professional and right-hand man. Only eight matches out of twenty-eight were won and six were lost, with fourteen drawn. Duckworth obligingly stood down at times to give a newcomer, Farrimond, a chance, and Paynter made rapid strides as an attractive and punishing batsman who could also field with relish and effect.

11. HISTORIC CENTURY

To prove his worth Paynter hit an historic century against Yorkshire at Bradford and for the first time Sibbles topped the hundred wicket figure and became the side's main bowler. Iddon joined the ranks of all-rounders by picking up seventy-six championship wickets and batting consistently, but Hopwood lacked his usual accuracy and it was left to a South African recruit, Gordon Hodgson, to partially fill the gap with fifty welcome wickets. It was a season of much experiment, with the introduction of a talented amateur in H. R. Butterworth and a promising professional of similar talent in Parkinson, but the plain fact remained that Lancashire could not fill the gaps created by the disappearance of McDonald, Dick Tyldesley or Hallows in one year or two. The season of 1933 proved the point. Nine matches were won and only one lost but there were eighteen draws disfiguring a record incapable of getting Lancashire and Eckersley back on top although Lord's had stepped up the winning award to a mammoth fifteen points. Vainly, they hoped to eliminate the many drawn games, but the English weather being what it is and professional cricketers what they are all the good off-the-field intentions counted for little when they were put into practice.

Wisely, Lancashire used the season to introduce new and

younger players. Among them were Washbrook, Hawkwood, Phillipson, Pollard and W. H. Lister, a talented Formby amateur earmarked to succeed Eckersley and given the opportunity to sample first-class cricket in advance. The weather, once May was out, provided batsmen with ideal conditions but Eckersley had too many learners under his command to hope for much more than moderate success. Phillipson and Washbrook made their début together. One came in as a fast bowler with the world at his feet; the other arrived as a batsman badly needed to bolster up the middle order. In point of fact, Phillipson, the bowler, looked the better batsman on his first appearance, but Washbrook put matters right in only his second match when he hit a splendid 152 off the Surrey bowling and was likened, not by Cardus, let it be said, to the one and only Johnny Tyldesley.

The season was a modest one for both newcomers, and for Washbrook there came a distressing episode when, swinging round against a Leicestershire bowler, he accidentally felled wicketkeeper Paddy Corrall and put him in hospital and out of the game for the rest of the summer. Lister came straight into the side from Cambridge University, where he had won a soccer blue but not a cricket one, and he impressed almost immediately with a punishing ninety-six out of 162 runs hit at Worcester in an hour of compelling batsmanship. Of the bowlers, Booth made the most progress, but when the auditors stepped in at the end of the season there was nothing really outstanding from any player – and that included the ageing Ernest Tyldesley and the slow-to-mature Paynter. It was generally agreed that much still remained to be done before Lancashire resumed their championship habits.

It was not so. Against all the odds Eckersley and his men triumphed once again in 1934, doing so on the strength of team work rather than an individual brilliance. Ernest Tyldesley hero-ically urged on the batsmen, and the bowling honours were shared between six men as thirteen games were won, fourteen drawn and only three lost. Men like Iddon, Hopwood, Watson, Duckworth and Sibbles provided the experience, along with the veteran Tyldesley, and runs were always forthcoming. Lacking a Mc-Donald or a Parkin, the attack was somewhat utilitarian but it was well varied and lacked nothing in effort or determination.

Sussex set the pace for most of the season but Lancashire's youthful brigade were learning fast and by late July were ready for a final swoop for honours. Only one victory had been won in the first seven championship matches, but the last seven were more important and more successful, and visits to Bristol, Worcester, Southampton and Nottingham were all crowned with victories that opened the way to the top. There was, however, a certain sourness about the Trent Bridge triumph, gained at much physical cost against the fast bowling of Larwood and Voce, and for a time relations between the counties were strained – not, it may well be mentioned, for the first time.

On good pitches Lancashire now found the pace of Phillipson and Pollard, and on more responsive ones the medium cutters of Sibbles backed by the left-handed spin of Iddon and Hopwood, were good enough to confuse even the strongest batting opposition. With Watson, Iddon, Paynter and Tyldesley still good for runs, and the young Washbrook occasionally coming to the rescue, Lancashire swept to the top and despite one or two alarms reached their goal. In paying tribute to a welcome revival the critics were mixed in their praises. Some considered the side lacked personality. Others wondered if the general level of first-class cricket was quite what it used to be. But the shrewd Cardus summed it more correctly when he pointed out that championships could not be won on luck alone and personalities took time to bloom. He looked beyond the batting and bowling averages but did not really class this Lancashire side with those that won so handsomely under Green. The game's most lyrical writer was right.

Events in 1935 proved the point. Lancashire failed to retain the championship, though playing some good cricket in winning twelve matches, drawing ten and losing six. Yorkshire stepped back on top as Eckersley and his men found it difficult to live up to their form and reputation of the previous summer. They slumped into fourth position but it was not difficult to find the reason why. Tyldesley and Iddon missed a lot of cricket through illness and Watson was surprisingly out of touch. Washbrook made steady progress. Paynter was spectacular at times but irritatingly inefficient at others. Oldfield arrived on the scene to display brilliant strokes and bring out the best of Cardus. Pollard and Phillipson maintained their promise and Sibbles and Booth continued to be reliable if not destructive bowlers. Duckworth was ever willing to step down and let the younger Farrimond feel his way as a wicketkeeper who could also get runs. Hopwood was an all-rounder of moods. He had done the highly creditable feat of capturing a hundred wickets and scoring a thousand runs in 1934, and he obliged again a year later. Yet there were times when a talented cricketer appeared to underestimate his power both as a run scorer and wicket taker. It was an attitude of mind that summed up a very ordinary season's cricket and crowd support dwindled in face of too much lack-lustre batting and far from penetrative bowling. The one factor relieving the gloom was the thought that most of the players, with Washbrook, Paynter and Oldfield among the batsmen, and Pollard and Phillipson in attack, were still on the threshold of their careers. In a word they were gaining vital experience.

After seven years as captain Eckersley turned from cricket to politics and fought a successful general election campaign to become Member of Parliament for the Exchange Division of Manchester in the winter of 1935. His cricketing days were over. Choice of successor rested between Lister and the senior professional Ernest Tyldesley. There were many who considered a break with tradition and the appointment of a professional as skipper to be essential in the formation of the new side. Lister had shown promise as a batsman and in the field. He, however, had no leadership experience and had volunteered to play under Tyldesley whenever Eckersley wanted a match off. The members were believed to be in favour of the long-serving and highly distinguished Tyldesley taking over but the decision rested with the committee and they voted 11-6 in favour of Lister and the age-old tradition of having an amateur in charge. That Tyldesley was prepared to turn amateur did not, apparently, impress and it occasioned no great surprise when a magnificent batsman and cricketer finally announced his retirement after only a couple of games under the new captain. At the age of forty-seven he could not be denied a well-earned rest and his record, on and off the field, was later burnished by distinguished service on the club committee as the first professional ever to be elected to such heights.

Tyldesley's retirement was not the only problem Lister had to solve. Watson's skill was on the wane and Sibbles was handicapped by a painful arm injury. Duckworth had lost his appetite for the game and was unhappy at the thought of keeping the brilliant Farrimond out of regular first-class cricket. Inevitably the position saw 'Ducky' lose his edge, and with both Iddon and Hopwood out of touch for most of the summer only seven championship games were won in 1936. The side was beaten six times and seventeen games were drawn in what proved to be another very ordinary season, although the still small crowds gained compensation by the brilliance of Paynter, Oldfield and Washbrook at times.

Not since 1904 had Lancashire cricket been so unsuccesful and a final placing at eleventh in the championship table brought no rejoicing, the unfortunate Lister reaping some severe criticism. He had a modest batting average of twenty and distinguished himself only with a century at Lord's that led to one of Lancashire's rare victories over Middlesex. Booth and Parkinson fell from grace and with the weather far from suitable for either spectators or players there was no great regret when a poor season ended. Lister bravely remained silent in face of the critics and expressed his willingness to carry on in 1937, although well aware of the problems and the demand for new blood from both the pavilion side and the public terraces.

In many respects Lister's second season in charge was a vital one. He needed to rebuild and yet could not do without the experience of players like Sibbles, Iddon and Booth. Sibbles was again handicapped by arm trouble but took 107 wickets. A Whitsuntide defeat by Yorkshire at Old Trafford reacted against the captain's desires and good intentions and of the thirty-two championship fixtures played, nine were won, eighteen drawn and five lost. It was an improvement upon the doleful 1936 season but still not good enough to make Lancashire either attractive or successful exponents of first-class cricket. Two newcomers, Place, a dour batsman from the Lancashire League, and Wilkinson, a talented bowler from the prolific Bolton area, made their débuts.

Nutter, a Merseyside recruit, was also given a chance and all was not lost. Paynter provided much of the better cricket that was forthcoming in brighter weather and Washbrook settled in as one of the most punishing and promising batsmen in the country. Alongside him Oldfield was maturing slowly, and with the ball Phillipson and Pollard were gradually assuming control and consistency. But it was the batsmen who did most to keep the still small crowds happy in what was yet again a season without much distinction for both Lancashire and the captain.

Since their championship success in 1934 Lancashire's side had undergone many changes, and when the 1938 season began both Duckworth and Sibbles were missing. The dynamic little wicket keeper had decided his future lay in the press box, and Sibbles, unable to find a cure for his arm injury, decided he could not carry on. Not for the first time the side had everything to gain and little to lose as long as they stuck by their young players. With Paynter producing his best form, Lancashire moved up the table to occupy the fourth position in the final reckoning. They had led the way for several weeks at one stage of a summer that produced many hard and fast wickets, and with Paynter dominating the batting and Wilkinson filling the spinning gap in sensational manner, fourteen matches were won against twelve drawn and six lost. Pollard and Phillipson had settled into an aggressive combination with the new ball and Nutter came along to render stout support whilst there was still some shine on the ball. But the bowler who made the real difference was Wilkinson.

This gangling youngster was another product of the Bolton League. Carefully nursed from his début in 1937, Wilkinson was in his element on pitches that gave him pace off the pitch. His ability to spin the ball was prodigious. He had big hands and utilised them well. His leg-break really fizzed off the pitch at times and his top-spinner trapped many an unwary batsman, playing back somewhat uncertainly. But it was the newcomer's googly that impressed most. He disguised it artfully, pitched it perfectly, and seldom strayed from the right line. His reward was a fantastic 145 wickets in his first season. They cost him nearly twenty-three runs each but Lancashire could well afford to pay this price. In point of fact it was cheap for a bowler of his kind

Master bowler, S. F. Barnes, at the height of his career

Old Trafford in 1946; Brian Sellers (Yorkshire) on the left, and Jack Fallows (Lancashire) on the right, inaugurate 'roses' cricket again after the war

Winston Place (*left*) and Cyril Washbrook, opening batsmen for Lancashire in the years immediately after the war

Above, Roy Tattersall
Lancashire's master
bowler from 1948 to
1960

R. W. Barber, the
1960-61 captain

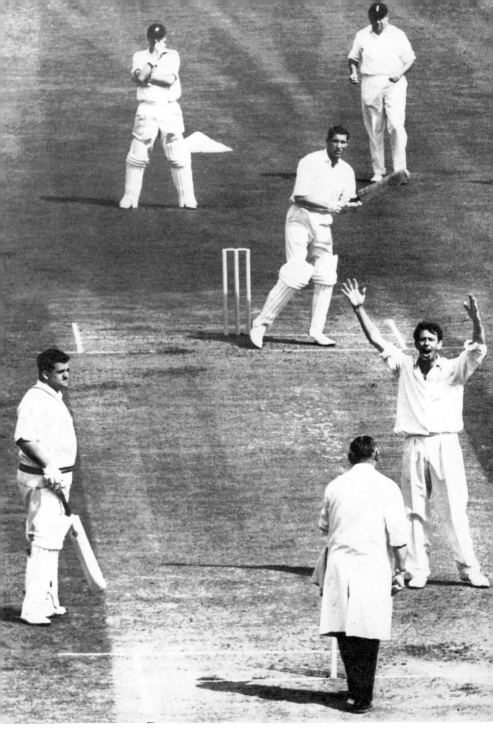

A cricketing milestone. Brian Statham, Lancashire and England fast bowler, claims South Africa's Tiger Lance as his 250th test victim at the Oval in 1965

and Wilkinson not only won his county cap but gained a place in the MCC side representing England in South Africa during the winter.

Without a doubt the lanky Wilkinson ranked as Lancashire's most important cricketing discovery in years, while alongside the newcomer, Paynter was always in top batting gear. The little left-hander was well established in the England side by this time and his fielding matched his batsmanship in the estimation of the crowds that still travelled to Old Trafford. Each weekend when Lister's men were at home Old Trafford would accommodate ten thousand or so, but there was a marked falling off in support during the week. This, however, was more a reflection on the economic state of the public rather than any great loss of interest, although of course, the Lancashire leagues were at the time going great guns and possessed a far bigger following than did the county side – a fact which the powers that be at Old Trafford failed to recognise. Many of them thought Lancashire cricket began and ended at Old Trafford. It did not, and whilst relationship between the two spheres was amiable enough on the surface there was no real desire to work together.

But back to the efforts Lister and his men made to re-establish form and reputation. An injury to Phillipson handicapped the side for a time and it was then that Nutter did his best work and, with Washbrook and Oldfield scoring consistently and attractively alongside the dashing Paynter, Lancashire were an attractive side to watch. It is true that Iddon and Hopwood failed to reach their best form, but such was the spirit and the strength of the side that their failures were of little consequence in a season that clearly indicated that the rebuilding, begun after the 1934 championship, had been successful. Knocking on the door of the senior team were promising cricketers in Place, Ikin and Roberts. Farrimond, too, had taken over from Duckworth to do a vital job efficiently. This little fellow, yet another Bolton League recruit, had actually been on two MCC tours, to South Africa and the West Indies, whilst still deputy to Duckworth in the county side, and his 'promotion' was in no way tinged with risk or doubt. Farrimond was a patient man, and whilst waiting for the call to arms, as it were, had more or less 'bossed' the large and busy

73

groundstaff Lancashire employed with Makepeace as coach. Disappointed a little at losing their grip after being at the top for a time, Lister and his men had accomplished much in 1938 and were well placed to challenge again in 1939. Unfortunately it was not to be. The weather was bad and the constant threat of Hitler and his German hordes made it hard to concentrate on cricket; nevertheless, ten championship matches were won, fourteen drawn, six lost – and the last one abandoned when war was declared.

Again Phillipson and Pollard proved themselves one of the liveliest and most aggressive opening pair of bowlers in the country, but conditions were all against Wilkinson repeating his phenomenal success of the previous season. He had been working hard for the MCC and England in South Africa throughout the winter and came home more than a little stale. His spin was still vicious at times and his length and direction remained remarkably consistent. Yet he failed to get to the hundred wicket mark and was expensive at times. But there could be no questioning the quality of Washbrook and Oldfield. Along with Paynter they provided the bulk of the runs, although Iddon had a much better season and Place did enough to suggest that he had what it took to slot into the side and strengthen it. Roberts, a left-hand spinner, and Ikin, a left-handed all-rounder from the Staffordshire League, were also competing for places, and Garlick was on hand when there was any off-spinning to do. Lister was frequently called away from cricket to fulfil his territorial training and T. A. Higson, son of the club chairman was drafted in to lead the side although Iddon had shown he was quite capable of taking charge. So bad was the weather at times that on one occasion the Lancashire and Warwickshire players decided to cut a pitch on the practice ground in a desperate effort to play. Alas, even that got waterlogged before a ball could be bowled; and that was the story of a season played under clouds of two kinds – rain and war. Yet there were times when the cricket sparkled, and Pollard followed a hat-trick against Glamorgan at Preston with ten wickets against Surrey before the game and cricket itself was abandoned for five long and arduous years of war that turned the world upside down.

Part Two

The war years to the present day

12. AN ARMY DEPOT

Old Trafford was quickly requisitioned as an army depot with
the Royal Engineers occupying the ground and buildings and the
majority of the staff, playing and administrative, taking up uniform and arms and suffering inevitable losses. Notable among
the casualties was P. T. Eckersley, killed in action very early in
the conflict against Hitler and his allies. Manchester was a target
for the Luftwaffe bombers and Old Trafford was blitzed at the
beginning of 1941 with damage to the pavilion and bomb craters
on the field of play. In due course the army moved out but Old
Trafford was still in demand for wartime purposes and the
Ministry of Supply took over to use the ground as a dump for
vehicles and equipment so necessary to the fighting forces. Administration continued on a smaller scale. Captain Rupert
Howard, the secretary when war broke out, was able to keep an
eye on things from a military posting nearby. The captain, promoted to major during the war, willingly sacrificed his leisure
hours and even his meal times to attend to essential cricketing
duties, working from the city centre office of the club chairman
and thankfully accepting subscriptions from loyal members determined to ensure that Lancashire would be ready to resume
cricketing hostilities when military ones were ended.

Leading players, almost all of them in uniform, found opportunity for an occasional game in aid of war charities, and although
Old Trafford was unavailable, the leagues and clubs of the
county, who kept going with remarkable dedication, staged games
that kept alive interest at both playing and spectator level. In
point of fact quite a lot of money was raised in these Red Cross

matches and two Lancashire committee members, Dr J. B. Holmes and G. S. Cadman, did a great job of work sponsoring matches and fielding teams under their colours.

Towards the end of the winter of 1944-5 the Lancashire committee, seriously depleted by other duties, were meeting again to plan for a resumption of first-class cricket, and although there were many obstacles in the way Old Trafford was available when, in 1945, a series of victory tests was arranged as a prelude to a resumption of full-scale county cricket in 1946. Several one-day games and an occasional two-day one had been played on the county ground before an England eleven met a strong Australian services eleven in one of the victory tests to usher in the big-time again at the Lancashire headquarters. England beat the Australians by six wickets; happily playing a leading part, on leave from the air force and the army, were Pollard and Phillipson. Despite the inconvenience of damaged stands and untenable seating, over seventy-two thousand spectators crammed Old Trafford over the three days of the match and receipts topped the £11,000 mark. Here was proof, if any was needed, that cricket was still a popular sport.

Throughout the following winter, the Lancashire committee, with the remarkable T. A. Higson as chairman, planned feverishly for a return to normal cricket and took their full share in discussions at Lord's and elsewhere to ensure that resumption of play should go as smoothly as possible. Without exception, every county had suffered blows. Wisely it was agreed there be no barriers to recruitment. Qualification rules were eased and even scrapped at times, and Lancashire, building a new side around Washbrook, Pollard, Phillipson, Wilkinson and Place, sought far and wide for the men to usher in the new era. They signed King, a Yorkshire batsman who played with Worcestershire, Brierley, a wicketkeeper from Glamorgan, and G. A. Edrich, a member of a fighting cricketing family from Norfolk, to play alongside their own players who had come through the war unscathed. The captaincy provided a problem. Lister was unable to resume a playing career and T. A. Higson could not afford the time. There was talk of Iddon turning amateur to take charge but, tragically, he was killed in a road accident a few weeks before the 1946 season opened. Eventually choice fell upon J. A. Fallows, son of the club treasurer, and a man with a good military record, even if his cricket had previously been played only at club and minor county level. Fallows took charge amid some criticism but he did a magnificent job although he could not call upon Oldfield, Nutter or Farrimond, who decided against returning to Old Trafford in view of what they considered unrealistic financial terms and better prospects elsewhere. Paynter took a similar attitude, although in his case he feared that the physical demands more than the cash ones would be too much of a handicap.

Of the 1939 team, Washbrook, Place, Pollard and Phillipson soon settled in again. Unfortunately, Wilkinson, who had spent the war in remote outposts and played little cricket, could not recapture his form and, although given every chance, faded from the scene without taking more than the odd wicket. Place stepped up to make Washbrook an ideal opening partner and Ikin fitted into the number three spot with stylish ease. King and Edrich added middle-order power and Wharton, a youngster from the leagues, also proved his ability. Roberts bowled well in support of Phillipson and Pollard, and with Garlick off-spinning profitably and Price emerging as a promising left-hander, Lancashire under Fallows might well have won the championship but for bad luck with the weather and the toss late in the season. Travelling conditions were spartan and hotels badly in need of refurnishing. Food was still rationed but Fallows cheerfully blended the side into a fighting cricketing unit. He contributed little with the bat but held his catches and accepted advice from his senior professionals, with Washbrook and Pollard his 'inner cabinet'. Fallows' real strength lay in his off-the-field activities. His main concern at all times was for the comfort of his team. He seldom failed to sort out a hotel manager and beg a few favours from both the room and food point of view, and he excelled himself one morning in a certain London hotel when, with only four fresh eggs available for twelve players and a scorer, he ended all arguments with the wisdom of a Solomon. 'We are in the field this morning. Let the bowlers have the eggs . . . the batsmen can have them tomorrow.' A simple solution, yet an important one, and typical of Fallows at all times!

Although Pollard was still in the army, he played enough cricket to become the accepted bowling spearhead, even if it was Price, a young left-hand spinner from Middleton, who topped the averages to earn a place in a test trial at Canterbury in his first season. With most county grounds suffering from a lack of attention during the war years, the pitches varied from the reasonably good to the downright bad and Lancashire were able to 'carry' two left-handers in Roberts and Price. Roberts, in point of fact, bowled his spinners at a brisk pace and did not utilize flight to the extent that Price did. Both were often employed together without detriment to results. The two left-handers, along with Phillipson and Pollard and occasional help from Garlick and Ikin, made up a strong Lancashire attack and with Washbrook in magnificent form with the bat few counties made the comeback to the first-class game as assuredly as did Lancashire.

Washbrook started the postwar period with a return of 1,475 runs from championship matches and was always in demand for England when the tests against India came along. He averaged almost seventy-four runs an innings and began an association with Hutton that was to sustain England at top cricketing level for several years. Place plodded along and made a name for himself as a dependable batsman, able to score steadily on good wickets and fight hard on bad ones. It was generally admitted that, although overshadowed by his more fashionable colleague, Place was the better batsman technically when it came to opposing bowlers with the elements in their favour. In the end, Yorkshire were champions but Lancashire had nothing to fear from any side on the field. It was off it where the county lacked flair and the sacking of Fallows in favour of Ken Cranston, after just one season in charge, had a disastrous effect on the side.

13. IN THE WILDERNESS

It was not so much the decision to replace a popular skipper but the manner in which it was done that had deep repercussions and led to years in the wilderness for Lancashire and their championship hopes. Just as the season ended, Fallows learned through a press leakage that he had been deposed and it hurt him deeply. What was even more important was its effect on the players he led. They saw in the manner of his dismissal a complete lack of regard for their own feelings and performances. In a day, doubts were sowed in their minds about their own security. If the captain could be summarily sacked, so could the professionals; at least, that was the way they looked at things and it opened a gulf between players and committee which widened as the years passed by until it reached the stage when there was almost open rebellion between those who administered and those who played. Nobody questioned the new skipper, Cranston's right to step into first-class cricket. The Liverpool man was a talented batsman and a splendid seam bowler who almost accomplished an eventful cricketing double in his first season. But he had no experience of leadership, or in man management, and although he was outwardly on good terms with the professionals he was never encouraged to seek the advice they alone could give him. Instead, he tended to rely on well meant but obviously unskilled guidance from the committee room. The fortunes of a side that had reopened so promisingly in just missing the championship, and providing three players, Washbrook, Pollard and Ikin, for the MCC tour of Australia and New Zealand, slumped badly. It was not that Cranston lacked support. In 1947 and 1948 Washbrook and Place were in superb form. They rivalled Compton and Edrich from the run-scoring point of view, and although Price faded from the scene because of the absence of skilled leadership, the bowlers, notably Pollard and Phillipson, were doing well enough in 1947 when thirteen championship games were won against eleven drawn, one tied and only one defeat.

Between them, Washbrook and Place gave their side many three figure starts and inflicted severe strain on Sussex with partnerships of 350 at Old Trafford and 233 at Eastbourne. Washbrook alone hit nine centuries, and with Ikin, G. A. Edrich and Wharton also batting consistently, Lancashire were seldom dismissed cheaply. Add the fact that Pollard claimed 131 wickets and even allowing for a slump on Phillipson's part it was clear that the side lacked nothing in ability. All it needed was the right kind of leadership. Cranston could not be expected to provide it. He batted delightfully and bowled successfully but it always was obvious there was no proper coordination of effort.

It was the same in 1948 when Bradman led the Australians triumphantly around the country. Washbrook and Place maintained form and reputation, Ikin, Wharton and Edrich contributed their full quota of runs, and so did the captain. Pollard flagged a little and so did Phillipson. In point of fact Phillipson faded from the scene and that season only eight championship matches were won against sixteen drawn and two lost. Two young amateurs, the brothers, N. D. and B. J. Howard, sons of the county secretary, appeared for the first time and showed promising form with the bat. Newcomers to the professional ranks were Hilton and Greenwood, two spin bowlers, who had also impressed, and the left-handed Hilton achieved fame by twice dismissing the mighty Bradman in one match. There was no lack of distinction in Lancashire cricket, but there was also no real team spirit. Cranston remained a cricketer talented enough to win an England cap as well as a county one but he had no pretensions to leadership and never pretended otherwise.

Cranston had in fact made it quite plain that he could only afford to stay on the scene for a brief period and at the end of 1948 he announced his intention of concentrating on his dentistry practice in Liverpool. Again the question of the captaincy presented problems. The obvious choice was Washbrook. There was no more experienced cricketer in the country and none more fitted for the job. But he was a professional, and as such had received a record £14,000 from his benefit in 1948. He gave no hint of a desire to turn amateur and Lancashire appointed N. D. Howard as skipper for 1949. In essence they ruined a promising batsman in an effort to make a successful captain. The youngster did his best but he was handicapped by the desire of certain officials to share his burden. It was often said, probably unfairly, that Howard took his instructions from three main sources – the club chairman, his father the club secretary, and his mother, a kindly soul with a deep love of cricket but no qualifications as a technical or tactical adviser. Howard's only chance was to listen to his experienced professionals but it was never apparent that he did. Indeed, he was often the recipient of messages and telegrams at home and away, containing instructions about what to do if he won the toss and when to make bowling changes. On one occasion a careless telephonist misheard and Howard received a telegram advising him to 'put Greenwood in first'. He duly did so, when what was meant was 'put Greenwood on first'. A distinction with a difference, and a state of affairs that could not help any cricketing cause.

Never once did any of the professionals criticise the young captain. They realised the awkwardness of his position and, rightly, they put the blame where it belonged – on the committee! Yet Howard had the courage to insist on the introduction of several youngsters who were to make an impact on the game. Roy Tattersall was one and Brian Statham was another. Tattersall was given his baptism in 1948 but Statham did not come on to the scene until 1950 when Pollard had followed Phillipson into league cricket and Garlick had joined Northamptonshire.

In 1949, under Howard, Lancashire finished in the lower half of the table and won only six championship matches, drew thirteen and lost seven, but there was no change in the leadership for the 1950 season although rumblings of discontent were to be heard on the members' enclosure and the popular side terraces. To his credit, Howard batted splendidly and fielded as well as anybody in the side. He often got runs when they were needed most and his ability as a player was never questioned. What is more, he showed he was learning as he went along, and, with sixteen matches won, ten drawn and only two lost, Lancashire shared the championship with Surrey. They did so, however, without showing much flair or dignity, in view of a pre-season announcement that the heavy roller would not be used at Old Trafford. In consequence the pitches were always in favour of the bowlers, and even if Pollard had made way for the lively young Statham it was the spinners who reaped a rich harvest. Sussex, always on the receiving end against Lancashire, were beaten in a day at Old Trafford when Hilton and Greenwood made life a misery for their batsmen. Under helpful conditions Tattersall had a great summer picking up 163 wickets for 12 runs each, and with

Hilton also topping the hundred wicket mark the batsmen had an easy time. None the less Washbrook averaged more than fifty runs an innings and encouraged his batting colleagues to score at a brisk rate throughout the season. They did so well that Edrich, Place, Ikin, Howard and a new Australian recruit, Grieves, all topped the thousand run mark.

Yet Lancashire were always regarded with suspicion that year because of the way in which they prepared their own pitches. A joint share of the championship was no real consolation. A change of policy, and let it be said the players were never once consulted, saw the heavy roller introduced in 1951, and Lancashire toppled, with only eight championship victories against eighteen draws and two defeats. Hard to beat but never difficult to contain, the side saw Tattersall, Statham, Hilton and Ikin called upon to play for England, and produced five batsmen with more than a thousand runs to their name. Washbrook and Place, of course, led the way, but Edrich was as consistent as ever and rivalled Place as a fighter second to none when the pitches proved difficult. Ikin and Grieves also reached four-figure aggregates but only Hilton topped the hundred wicket mark.

Once again there was a clear lack of coordination of brilliant individual efforts into teamsmanship, and Howard's captaincy was yet again the topic of critical comment around the ring. The committee ignored it. The youngster was reappointed and had in point of fact led England and the MCC in India and Pakistan during the winter with Tattersall, Hilton and Statham also in the side. No county had more promising recruits, but still success eluded them and in 1952 Lancashire were placed third behind Surrey and Yorkshire with a record of twelve wins, twelve draws, three defeats and one tied game. All the main batsmen topped the thousand mark again and Wharton joined the élite in this field. With Statham and Tattersall taking more than a hundred wickets each and Hilton not far behind again there was ample evidence of considerable ability but no team cohesion. Howard, as always, secured trials for any youngster of real promise but crowd support dwindled and the gulf between committee and players was wider than ever as Lancashire endured rather than enjoyed playing cricket.

Howard had been handicapped by illness at times throughout the 1952 season and Lancashire did not hesitate to ask Washbrook to take command. The England batsman was by now one of the most experienced and highly respected in the game, but the authority he displayed with the bat never really showed itself from the leadership point of view, although, of course, he commanded respect and often set problems for the opposition by his shrewd handling of bowlers and setting of fields. There was talk of Howard standing down at the end of the summer, but the committee reappointed him and with the bowling as good as any in the country, bar Surrey's, there were high hopes of the championship in 1953 when the Australians were touring and test match calls were thought likely to hit other counties more than Lancashire. In the event, things did not work out that way. Surrey retained the championship and Lancashire again finished in third position behind Sussex, with the knowledge that the season had again proved the point, so often made, that the side possessed some talented cricketers but collectively they lacked what it takes to make the most of the ability available. Statham bowled steadily throughout the summer but Tattersall was the only bowler to top the hundred wicket mark and, for a change, Grieves led the batsmen with Edrich and Washbrook close behind but with Place showing signs of strain. Not for the first time Lancashire and Howard had to ponder the presence of two left-handed spinners in Hilton and Berry. Both were good enough to win England caps, yet were too similar in style and pace to give the variety so badly needed.

14. LACK OF SUPPORT

There was, too, a lack of support for Statham with the new ball, but the season was not without its impressive victories and none was more publicised than when they went to Bath to beat Somerset with fifty-nine minutes to spare on the first day of Bertie Buse's benefit match. Tattersall, with match figures of 13-79, made the best possible use of a suspect pitch and after

Somerset had been shot out for fifty-five before lunch Lancashire replied with 158 before tea and then ran through the home ranks again for seventy-nine runs to win by an innings.

Let it be noted that the best batting in this low-scoring game came from Marner, a youngster from the Central Lancashire League who had made his début the season before and now looked likely to clinch his place as a hard-hitting batsman who could bowl some brisk seamers and hold his catches both in the deep and closer to the wicket. Marner's innings of forty-four at Bath contained two sixes, a four and a two, in one over from Buse, and there could be no denying that the burly youngster lacked nothing in spirit as well as promise. For Buse there was compensation in a sensational one-day finish, for sympathisers up and down the country sent donations and what, at the time, appeared to be a disastrous benefit match did not turn out quite so badly after all.

Howard's leadership in 1953 showed signs of growing maturity but there were still times when a lack of application in the ranks prevented Lancashire from winning matches they had dominated and at the end of the season the young amateur decided he would have to concentrate on the calls of a family business. For five years Howard had struggled to master the intricate demands of cricket leadership and he had never spared himself in an effort to do the best he possibly could for Lancashire. He had sacrificed his own high ability as a batsman to help steer a side composed of several 'old sweats' and a bunch of youngsters through critical years. On paper, with a joint share of the championship his only success, he did not appear to have achieved much. But there was more to it than that. One of Howard's redeeming features was a willingness to give new players a chance. He believed in the old axiom that if they were good enough they were old enough. Perhaps the fact that he was pushed to the front very early in his own career lent credence to this point of view, but a talented young sportsman who also won county honours at hockey and golf can look back upon his captaincy period with a certain amount of pride. He had seen Tattersall, Statham, Hilton and Berry gain England caps as well as county ones under his leadership, and on the verge, as he stepped down, were other highly promising young players of the calibre of Marner, Pullar and Dyson.

Howard's decision to retire from both the captaincy and the first-class game at the age of twenty-eight was a blow. He had served Lancashire well but had been denied the full fruits of his labours by being handicapped too soon and too often. There were many at Old Trafford, players, committee and members alike, who considered Nigel Howard's considerable talents had been wasted. That was not so, and his record proves the point. That he would have done a great deal more had he been allowed to play, unfettered with captaincy cares, goes without saying. The plain fact remains that when he went, the county at once broke from tradition and appointed Washbrook as Lancashire's captain in readiness for the 1954 season. Had they taken a similar step five years previously, thus allowing Howard to mature in the ranks as it were, the whole history of the club might have taken a far less eventful course. Much more of a case could be made out for appointing Washbrook as leader in 1949 than in 1954. A master batsman, he was at the height of his form and fitness when Howard took over. It was no secret that the senior professional craved the job and would have dedicated himself to the task of leading the way. Even five years later Washbrook was still a very fine batsman and a cricketer beyond reproach. Never once in the whole of an illustrious career did he utter a wrong word or show one sign of bad cricketing manners, and when the call came, belated but inevitable, the old-timer played on in the vain hope that he could still do the sort of job he had envisaged when passed over the first time.

Let it be said at once, Washbrook was given more authority than most of Lancashire's postwar captains. As befitted a man with vast experience, playing matters and policies on the field were left almost entirely to him. Team selection was another matter, but Washbrook obviously had a bigger say than usual in this sphere, although there were times when it appeared that young players were not quite getting the opportunities they merited. The plain fact was that there remained a generation gap between the captain and the newcomers. Washbrook had first sampled county cricket in the day when professionalism called for a stern realization of discipline and custom; on his own admission he was seldom encouraged to voice an opinion in the dressing room until he won his county cap and even then only on the command of his captain or senior colleague. First-class cricket in the late 1930s demanded stern control and an appreciation of one's place in the scheme of things. No player was ever the worse for this sort of atmosphere, but the second world war did much to undermine the old ideals, and after the first flush of the new cricketing era before the 1940s were over, more and more youngsters came into the game with new ideas of what constituted life – in cricket or any other sphere!

The youngsters of those days were high-spirited and far more casual in their outlook on life and living and this was where Washbrook could not really find common ground with the new Lancashire players. He had been through a hard school himself and demanded the same sort of dedication, discipline and self-control he himself had always practised. He never once spared himself in the cause of Lancashire cricket and expected his men sternly to follow his example, so that he became, in a sense, a bogey man to the many newcomers Lancashire fielded in those rebuilding days. Place and Ikin were past their best and Pollard had gone. The captain was the only experienced postwar player still on Lancashire's active list and he tried desperately hard to see the point of view of the new generation, but instead of becoming a father figure he assumed, undoubtedly without being aware of it, the role of all-demanding schoolmaster. He never did anything, on the field or off it, which he considered detrimental to the game of cricket or Lancashire's part in it, and for five years Washbrook struggled against the odds trying to create a new Lancashire cricketing look without any real success. He had in Statham one of the best fast bowlers of any age, but it was not until Higgs came along in 1958 that Washbrook could offer a willing and tireless attacker the right kind of support at the start of an innings. Numerous men were tried in an effort to provide Statham with worthwhile support but none really made the grade until Higgs was discovered in Staffordshire League cricket and persuaded to try his luck at Old Trafford. With the bat Lancashire still relied a great deal upon Washbrook, but in

Pullar, Marner and Dyson they had promising recruits; Place and Ikin played less and less before eventually retiring and leaving their old colleague entirely on his own with a new bunch of post-war cricketers.

In Tattersall and Hilton he claimed two of the best spin bowlers in the country but Berry had gone, fearing that competition with Hilton was against his best interests. As always, however, when one man went another stepped up. In Lancashire's case the newcomer was the talented Greenhough, a leg spinner who showed promise of becoming as deadly as Wilkinson had been on his début before the war. In spite of their rebuilding demands, Lancashire, under Washbrook in 1954, appeared a strong combination, but only six championship matches were won against twelve drawn, three lost and seven 'no decisions' in a summer of much inclement weather. Only two batsmen, Washbrook and Wharton, topped the thousand run mark, and Tattersall alone had more than a hundred wickets. Statham with seventy-three victims and Hilton who had eighty-seven both contributed much against the odds but there was a lack of solidarity as well as sparkle about Lancashire cricket in Washbrook's first year as captain. He had seen R. W. Barber make his début as a highly talented schoolboy all-rounder and been impressed by the appearance of C. S. Smith as an amateur fast bowler destined to win a Cambridge blue. But Greenhough found the going hard on the slow pitches that abounded and Marner lost his chance because of a severe football injury that put him out of action for the whole of the summer. When all the facts and figures were added up, Lancashire finished tenth in the championship table and crowd support was at a new low level.

Things were little better in 1955. Again the team occupied a middle of the table position but four batsmen, Grieves, Washbrook, Ikin and Wharton, hit over a thousand runs and Edrich was not far behind. With the ball, Tattersall was as consistent as ever, with 105 wickets, but Statham, taking seventy-nine championship wickets for 12.84 runs each, still lacked consistent support with the new ball. Hilton chipped in with ninety-one victims but Greenhough could not command a regular place in the side because he lacked length and direction on pitches all against his kind of spin. It was also said that as a temperamental bowler he lacked encouragement, but Washbrook had many problems and Greenhough was one he put aside for the time being. Barber played when his term at Cambridge University had ended and so did Smith but trials for Goodwin and Standring still failed to find the man Statham and Lancashire so badly needed to share the new ball. Marner made a brief comeback after his injury and Bond's name appeared in the averages for the first time in a season that saw ten championship matches won against eight drawn, ten lost and one no decision. In a nutshell, little progress had been made and Old Trafford was far from a popular sporting venue.

15. MEMORABLE COMEBACK

Washbrook was finding the going hard but he cheerfully accepted reappointment although he had passed his fortieth birthday and had to give serious consideration to a career outside the game. Yet in 1956 Washbrook took Lancashire to the runners-up position behind Surrey, served as a test selector and made a memorable comeback to the England batting ranks in the last three tests against Australia. Frequently absent, but always a power behind the scenes, Washbrook saw his side win twelve of their twenty-eight championship matches, with twelve drawn, two no decisions and only two defeats. Wharton led the batting with 1,389 runs, with Grieves not far behind and Edrich again only just failing to reach the four-figure milestone.

Washbrook's contribution amounted to 861 runs in eighteen matches and when the skipper was away Lancashire lost nothing in leadership because of the thorough way Edrich assumed responsibility. Always a fighter, the Norfolk man had the rare gift of remaining one of the boys yet stepping up to boss the show without loss of prestige or dignity. The younger players leaned heavily on Edrich and whilst it would be unkind to say that Washbrook was not missed, there were compensating features about the side's cricket when Edrich was in command. Tattersall,

89

Statham and Hilton were again the main bowlers, but Hilton, free of test demands, was the only one to top the hundred mark. Greenhough had a better summer. He had better pitches and took 62 wickets at 17 runs or so each, and although Ikin faded from the scene Pullar made steady progress to contribute 935 runs, whilst Dyson, like Pullar, a Central Lancashire League recruit, hit 897 runs and won his county cap alongside Greenhough, wicketkeeper Jordan and amateur pace bowler C. S. Smith.

Bond, strangely enough, did not appear at all during the 1956 season and the talented Barber made only two trips to the wicket. Undoubtedly the highlight of an encouraging summer came when Leicestershire were beaten at Old Trafford without loss of one Lancashire wicket. Under Edrich's shrewd guidance Leicestershire were dismissed for 108, with Statham, Hilton and Greenhough sharing the wickets, and Lancashire replied with Wharton hitting eighty-seven and Dyson seventy-five in an unbroken opening partnership of 165 before Edrich, cannily assessing the weather prospects, declared and saw Hilton and Greenhough run through the opposition a second time for 122. Lancashire, set to hit sixty-six for victory, again got the runs through Wharton and Dyson without losing a wicket in a hectic chase against the clock and the weather.

It was a memorable victory, and the pavilion side critics were not slow to point out it had been achieved without Washbrook at the helm. It was one of the crosses Washbrook had to bear that he could do nothing right in the eyes of a minority of ever-critical club members. It was unfair and unsporting, and unfortunately the bulk of those who still supported Lancashire cricket failed to give the veteran full marks for his dedication to duty. After all, he was playing on against his own inclination in an effort to re-establish his county as a cricketing power.

Looking to the future, Lancashire decided that in 1957 Edrich should be allowed to concentrate on captaining the second team and help train on the many promising young players who were, at the time, being given trials. Fortunately Ikin, in his final season, regained form and fitness in contributing over a thousand runs, but it was Wharton, batting consistently to acquire 1,421 runs, who did much to ensure his side good starts. Washbrook, often absent on test selectorial duty, and Statham in regular demand by England, were both badly missed at times although the captain contributed 750 runs in the twenty-two matches he played and Statham claimed a hundred championship wickets at 12.57 each.

In all, ten out of twenty-eight championship matches were won, eight drawn and eight lost, and the remarkably consistent Tattersall again topped the hundred wicket mark, with Green-hough and Hilton well to the fore in the spin supporting roles. A good start to the season gave rise to high hopes, and under a new points system Lancashire gained a maximum seventy points from their first five championship games. Then came the tests and the frequent absence of the captain and the main bowler; the next five games brought no reward at all and Lancashire's title hopes faded. In the end they finished sixth, and although Pullar remained full of run-scoring promise, with 814 runs in nineteen matches, it was the old brigade of Wharton and Ikin that saw the season remained a fair one. Grieves, for once, lacked consistency, but Bond, given more encouragement, looked a good bet for the future. One of the contributory factors to an ordinary season was the absence of wicketkeeper Jordan, who missed half the pro-gramme through injury, thus giving a chance to Wilson in a key position. From the spectator point of view Lancashire were again in the doldrums, with few big crowds and the critical minority on the pavilion side again causing players some concern with remarks that frequently bordered on the aggressive and unseemly. For a club with Lancashire's fine sporting traditions this small bunch of super-critics was a source of worry to players and committee alike and some straight speaking at the club's annual meeting in the winter succeeded in abating the nuisance to a marked degree.

The long search for a worthwhile partner for Statham with the new ball was solved in 1958 when Higgs emerged to take sixty-two wickets and give the England bowler the sort of support he had so long craved. Washbrook used the new man wisely, and with Tattersall and Hilton still highly successful spin bowlers there was little wrong with the attack. Unfortunately the batting left much to be desired, although Pullar finally 'arrived' by topping the thousand mark for the first time, and Marner made a welcome and successful return to the side after injury to top the averages with 1,175 runs and produce several innings of outstanding merit. Aggressiveness was the keynote of Marner's success and for a youngster built on burly lines he raised hopes of tremendous seasons ahead. Barber, playing his first full season after completing his education at Cambridge also batted well to contribute 836 runs for an average of twenty-six, but Wharton, Grieves and Washbrook all struggled to get going and failed to reach the thousand mark. None the less, nine championship matches were won, eight drawn and seven lost; the side dropped one place in the championship table, from sixth to seventh, but gained compensation from the emergence of Higgs with the ball and Pullar and Marner as batsmen capable of attractive and compelling cricket. Crowd support showed signs of increasing but still left Old Trafford something of a sporting venue with a ghost-like air. Weekends usually saw a fair mustering of members and public but mid-week matches were often played in a funeral atmosphere. This state of affairs did not help Washbrook in his struggle to re-establish Lancashire as a power in the cricket world, but the old-timer soldiered on as a figure respected by the authorities but still more feared than admired by his players – the young ones in particular!

What was it prevented the barriers from being breached? Often accused of arrogance because of a militant swagger, Washbrook was far from a martinet. He could never, perhaps, accept the new permissiveness that was creeping into life and into cricket but the major reason for his apparent aloofness was undoubtedly the generation gap. He simply lacked the company and support of players brought up to the same iron discipline of his own days. And there was nothing anybody could do about it, for the skipper was at least ten years older than anybody else in the side. They were vital years. Feeling the strain, both mentally and physically, Washbrook allowed himself to be reappointed for the 1959 season and tried as hard as ever to lead the side to better things. He succeeded insofar as Lancashire moved up the table to occupy the fifth position by winning twelve, drawing nine and losing seven of their championship matches. The rapid progress made by Higgs as Statham's established first assistant, and far more consistent spin bowling by Greenhough covered up for remarkable falls from grace by both Tattersall and Hilton. After years of consistent spinning the right-hander from Bolton and the left-hander from Oldham completely lost touch and nothing was more remarkable than the failure of Tattersall who bowled only fifty-seven overs and took a mere five wickets before being dropped. Hilton had to be satisfied with twenty-nine victims and it was the beginning of the end for two fine bowlers. Statham suffered from strains in mid-season but still took ninety-seven wickets, and Higgs was only one short of the hundred mark in his second season of regular first-class cricket. Greenhough was responsible for the dismissal of ninety-three batsmen, and with Grieves regaining his batting touch and Pullar hitting three centuries against Yorkshire and emerging as an opening batsman of England class there was much merit about Lancashire's cricket in 1959.

Few other county sides could have offset the failure of Tattersall and Hilton so successfully, and with Barber batting consistently well and Bond also contributing some sound innings Washbrook, back to something like his best form with 940 runs, considered the time ripe to at last step down. He had been on the first-class cricket scene from 1933 to 1959 and retirement at the age of forty-four had been well earned. Lancashire had shown their gratitude with a record benefit award of £14,000 in 1948 and marked his departure as a player with a testimonial worth another £1,502 as well as making him a life member of the club and later electing him to committee status. Many tributes were paid as Washbrook passed from the cricketing scene. That he had been a magnificent batsman and a superb fieldsman nobody could or would contest. That he had also been the perfect professional was also beyond dispute. The one query against his name was his captaincy. He had not been a failure. Far from it. Yet he had not been a success. It was generally conceded that Washbrook had been kept waiting too long before being invited to lead the side. Had he been appointed ahead of Nigel Howard instead of after him, it was argued, Washbrook would have been as great a captain as he was a batsman. It is an assertion beyond proof. Let it suffice to be said that Cyril Washbrook never gave anything but his best in the cause of Lancashire cricket. No man can give more.

16. ANOTHER DIFFICULT CHOICE

Choice of a successor proved difficult yet again. The real amateurs, especially those with experience, were few and far between. Lancashire again had the choice of asking a young and inexperienced amateur in Barber to take over, or allowing one of the more senior professionals to take over. What happened to the plan to let Edrich concentrate on the second team leadership? The minor county man did a magnificent job in preparing such players as Pullar, Marner, Dyson, Jordan, Clayton and Greenhough for stardom, but he was somewhat mysteriously dismissed from the staff in 1958. Various reasons were advanced for his sudden departure but the plain truth lay in the fact that Edrich refused to name one or two of his young charges who had indulged in some high spirited junketing on a second team trip. He accepted full responsibility, as all good captains should – and he paid the price. Had Edrich stayed and succeeded Washbrook, Lancashire cricket would have bloomed gloriously, because he had tended the garden so well. The youngsters worshipped him. They admired his fighting qualities and his desire to share their joys on and off the field. It was one of the many tragedies of Lancashire cricket that Geoff Edrich was not allowed to complete the job he set out to do at Old Trafford. Be that as it may, Lancashire again committed the error of sacrificing the career of a talented all-round cricketer by saddling him with the captaincy before he was ready for it. Bob Barber was appointed to succeed Washbrook, and in order to 'help' the young left-hander master an arduous task the committee decided he should not stay with the professionals on tour. They turned the clock back some twenty years by booking their captain in at a different hotel and segregating him from the professionals except on the field and in the dressing room.

In theory Lancashire could claim this was a system predominantly successful between the two world wars. What they did not take into account was the new way of life and the new freedom of the individual that had come to be accepted as the 1960s took over from the 1950s. Barber, to his credit, made every effort to win the team's confidence, but he was handicapped by a lack of authority and an even greater unawareness of how the professional cricketer thought and lived. Wharton would have been a better choice, and Grieves was also on hand. Both had long experience of first-class cricket and each was popular with the youngsters now being freely drafted into the side. Team spirit was good, but, as was the case when Howard took over, it degenerated with the senior professionals ignored and the younger ones forgotten. Unable to live with his men, Barber was a sad and lonely young cricketer in his first year as captain. It is his own secret whether he was told where and when to seek advice, but the plain fact remains that he seldom sought to untangle knotty cricketing problems with his senior professionals; and when reprimands were needed they came from the committee, not the captain.

Yet Barber had the satisfaction of leading a successful side. Yorkshire were beaten twice, at Leeds and Old Trafford, and the August bank holiday victory raised high hopes of the championship to come; but Barber's lack of experience led him to severe criticism of Cowdrey's captaincy when Kent avoided defeat after Yorkshire had been beaten. Unwisely insisting upon making his views on Cowdrey public, the Lancashire captain came up against criticism from the men who had appointed him – the club committee.

In addition, the loss of four out of the last six championship matches saw Yorkshire retain the title, Dyson dismissed, Clayton dropped and Wharton allowed to leave for Leicestershire. The season ended in what was akin to open warfare between the professionals and their young captain, with the committee split down the middle following the criticism of Cowdrey and Kent. Fortunately, Statham had had a magnificent season, with ninety-seven wickets for Lancashire and more for England. Greenhough had also gained test caps in returning figures of 111 wickets at 18.23 each, and Higgs had maintained form and fitness in his usual consistent manner by picking up 110 victims. What is more, Barber, using himself sparingly as a bowler, still managed to dismiss forty-seven batsmen of reasonable rate and there was nothing wrong with the Lancashire attack in a season that saw thirteen championship matches won, ten drawn and eight lost. A glance at the batting averages revealed Pullar, Grieves, Barber, Wharton and Marner had all topped the thousand run mark.

There could be no denying the talent of the players, young and old alike. What was lacking was the right kind of leadership. Once again the fault was not Barber's alone. The circumstances and the conditions under which he took over never gave him a real chance of success. Yet he came so near to it – and was reappointed for the following season. It proved to be a disastrous one. Lancashire slumped to thirteenth place in the championship table, winning eleven matches, drawing eighteen and losing eight, in a summer when neither batsmen nor bowlers reached their full potential. The absence of Wharton left a hole, but Pullar was now well established and with Bond at last topping the thousand run mark and Barber, Grieves and Booth doing the same, big totals were not unknown. Statham, frequently on England duty, was still the bowler who mattered most, with seventy-eight wickets, but Higgs was too costly, although dismissing ninety-five batsmen. Greenhough suffered something of a decline because of injuries to fingers and feet. The Rochdale leg-spinner took only twenty-six victims, but Colin Hilton, a pace bowler from the Atherton area, bowled admirably on occasions, making a good deputy for Statham, and picking up sixty-five wickets at a reasonable rate. Barber, always a reluctant bowler, took forty wickets, and would have had more if he had worked harder. Once again individual talent could not be harnessed into teamwork and for once Lancashire were lackadaisical in the field. Far too many batsmen were allowed to run twos instead of singles and anticipation for both catches and strokes left much to be desired. Towards the end of the campaign Barber was not only tired of the job but plainly irritated by it. His skills were undoubtedly high, but he was not enjoying his cricket and therefore not making the best use of either his own or his team's capabilities. Belatedly, the committee announced that in Barber's own interests and in the cause of his own development they were to relieve him of his captaincy duties for the 1962 season. A gamble had failed. Barber, like Howard, had sacrificed some of his natural ability in the vain hope of making a good captain.

Barber took his demotion with good sportsmanship and agreed to stay on and play under a new man. Grieves, however, decided it was time he looked elsewhere for a living and went into the Central Lancashire League and business. Finding the man to take over was again the prime occupation of a harassed committee in the winter months and many and varied were the suggestions put forward. There was talk of Howard returning, of Washbrook being recalled, and even of asking Statham to undertake the leadership as well as do the bulk of the bowling. Speculation was rife. It was eventually ended with the announcement that J. F. Blackledge had accepted an invitation to captain Lancashire in 1962.

Who was the new man? He had played no first-class cricket but had enjoyed an occasional game with the county second team and done well in Northern League cricket. He was recommended to Lancashire as a young man with a flair for the game. It was also said he possessed the mysterious something that would enable him to lead men. Again it was a tragic mistake. Lancashire, under Joe Blackledge, endured their worst ever season, winning only two championship matches, losing sixteen and managing to avoid defeat fourteen times. The new skipper could not be blamed for everything that went wrong. He started off by having to be introduced to each member of the side and ran into trouble through injury and illness almost from the first match. He could seldom win the toss and when he did his batsmen were usually lacking in enterprise and authority. As the season wore on, things got worse instead of better and in August there were five occasions when the whole side failed to reach the hundred. Four of the failures came in two matches with double collapses against Gloucestershire and Somerset, highlighting the extent of a slump unprecedented in Lancashire cricketing history. Yet five batsmen, Pullar, Bond, Marner, Barber and Booth, topped the thousand run mark. No bowler reached the hundred mark and even Statham was below par with seventy-seven wickets costing him twenty-three runs each. Hilton did well with eighty-seven victims but Higgs was ineffective with sixty and for the first time Lever's name appeared in the averages with twenty wickets, although he paid over thirty runs each for them. Greenhough suffered in the general decline and Barber was out of touch as a bowler although always the side's best fieldsman. Blackledge, of course, had the critics howling for his blood. His return with the bat was a modest 548 runs for an average of 15 and as he was by no means an agile fielder the new Lancashire captain had a nightmare of a season. He was to be pitied rather than blamed. Those who nominated him were sadly lacking in the knowledge of what leadership in first-class cricket demanded and the experiment proved a ghastly failure. Not only were playing returns bad but the effect on the team was almost incalculable as Blackledge expressed an earnest wish to retire from the scene.

There was no pressure on him to stay and once again the winter months were dominated by committee deliberations about his successor. To complicate matters Barber had finally reached the end of his patience with the club and its administrators. He was allowed to go, and eventually he joined Warwickshire where he soon blossomed as a highly entertaining cricketer when unfettered by responsibilities. Plainly in a dilemma, Lancashire solved the captaincy problem by recalling Grieves from Stockport but injuries to Pullar and Bond completely upset the balance of the side the Australian was asked to lead. A knee injury sustained with England in Australia compelled Pullar to miss all but thirteen matches, and with Bond injured and suffering a broken arm against the West Indies at Old Trafford only two batsmen, Marner and Grieves, topped the thousand run figure. Statham returned to his best form with 101 victims but Higgs was still out of touch and Hilton became dissatisfied and eventually migrated to Essex. Lever became a useful aid for Statham with fifty-seven wickets, and Greenhough, also topping the half-century mark, did his best in the spinning line without doing much to improve things. Winning only four championship matches and drawing thirteen, with ten lost, Lancashire moved up one place – from sixteenth to fifteenth – and Old Trafford was well and truly in the cricketing doldrums!

17. CENTENARY BLUNDER

Constant and often bewildering team changes complicated the
task Grieves so willingly undertook. Among the new names ap-
pearing were Pilling and Sullivan. Dyson returned to the staff
after a spell in Scottish cricket but he did little, and all in all the
end of the season came as a relief to all – especially to Grieves,
who knew that if he and Marner failed with the bat recovery was
generally beyond the power of those that followed. Grieves was
reappointed to lead again in 1964, the club's centenary year, but
any hope of vast improvement was soon dispelled. In point of
fact, the season proved a turbulent one with repercussions on and
off the field. Only four matches were won against ten lost and
thirteen drawn, and Grieves saw his side finish fourth from the
bottom in a welter of speculation about his own future and that
of several other leading players. Following a poor display against
Warwickshire in the semi-final of the new Gillette Cup competition when Old Trafford housed its biggest crowd in years –
over twenty thousand saw the game – the club's cricket committee decided to dispense with the services of Clayton and
Marner 'in the best interest of Lancashire cricket', not to re-
engage Dyson, and to terminate Grieves's contracts as captain.
They made their decision three weeks before the end of the
season and tried to keep it a secret.

In the end there was an inspired press leakage during the
course of the county's 'celebration' match with an MCC team,
and the upshot was an eventual uprising against the committee.
In spite of the difficulties, there were signs of an improvement on
the field. Two university blues, D. M. Green and D. R. Worsley,
from Oxford, had been tempted to become contracted players
after occasional appearances as amateurs, and Green at once
impressed as a hard-hitting batsman with over a thousand
runs to his name in his first season. Worsley, a studious left-
hander, totalled 747 in his first full summer, and with Pullar
almost back to his best and Marner and Grieves also top-

ping the thousand run mark Lancashire built up some useful totals.

With the ball Statham was again in good form, with 103 victims, but the somewhat bold experiment of bringing Sonny Ramadhin into championship cricket, after years in the leagues, was only partially successful. The West Indies spin bowler took eighty wickets in his first season but Higgs and Greenhough were again ineffective and Lever got few chances. The decision to engage Ramadhin at the age of thirty-four was all the more remarkable because of Lancashire's refusal to consider another overseas-born player who had done remarkably well in league cricket and could offer batting as well as bowling capabilities to the first-class scene. His name was Basil D'Oliveira and Lancashire's loss was Worcestershire's gain!

Another desperate gamble that failed was the appointment of Washbrook as the club's first-ever team manager. The intention was that the old-timer should take some of the responsibility load off Grieve's shoulders and also act as a brake on the high spirits of several of the younger players who were apt to enjoy themselves too boisterously at times.

To complicate matters still more, Geoffrey Howard, the club secretary, decided to return to Surrey and a bunch of members demanded the inevitable showdown, with a call for a special meeting and a vote of no confidence in the committee. That, however, is an episode dealt with elsewhere and let it suffice to say that Lancashire ended their centenary season in a welter of criticism, uncertainty and near rebellion. Out of chaos was to come order but the winter was a long and difficult one, with the committee reaping even more criticism by advertising in *The Times* for a new captain. It was, of course, a winter of feverish activity and it ended with a completely new look on the field and off. The captaincy problem was solved by a down-to-earth approach and the appointment of Statham to succeed Grieves. The new people on the committee were realists. They knew the value of Statham and placed their faith in him. Never for one moment did they underestimate the new demands made upon a long-serving and dedicated fast bowler. ' I will do my best ', was the promise made to the club when Statham was invited to occupy the hot seat.

No more. No less. But Lancashire's new administrators asked for nothing more.

They knew Statham, and they were confident he could do a good job. They were also aware that time was needed to repair the damaged fabric of playing resources. Experienced men had gone. Young newcomers had to be encouraged yet not embarrassed. Opportunity had to be matched with understanding. Trial periods had to be sympathetic ones, and with the dramatic change of control off the field came sweeping changes affecting the players. Charles Hallows was brought back to take charge of the coaching, with Norman Oldfield as his deputy. In a word, Lancashire placed their faith in Lancashire players at all levels. And so the 1965 season opened amid a welter of speculation. There were many who insisted that Statham could not combine his duties as the club's leading wicket-taker with those of the captaincy. Optimists and pessimists alike were warned not to expect too much too soon. The best that was anticipated was a revival of team spirit and some challenging cricket.

It was forthcoming, although in a season when only five championship matches were won against thirteen lost and nine drawn there was only a slight improvement in the team's final championship placing. One had to look deeper than actual results to see the shape of things to come. Statham shrugged off the captaincy burden with a magnificent return of 124 wickets at little over twelve runs each. Higgs returned to both form and fitness to capture 102 wickets, and Greenhough (fifty-four victims) and Lever (forty wickets) lent splendid assistance in none too good a summer from the weather point of view. With the bat, little Pilling made his first major impact with 963 runs and an average of over thirty, but it was Green who led the way with an aggregate of 1,784 and an average of more than thirty-four every innings. Pullar also topped the thousand mark and Snellgrove came along to hint at better things to come. Sullivan was also playing some useful cricket and Knox did by no means badly on his arrival from the north-east. Shuttleworth made a promising first-class cricket début but Ramadhin faded from the scene as the knowledgeable ones had forecast he would.

Slowly but surely, Statham and Lancashire were winning back

lost ground and lost spectators. The side had thrown off an air of resignation which suggested they endured rather than enjoyed their cricket and almost for the first time there were spontaneous signs of glee at the fall of a wicket or the hitting of a six. Years before it had been noted that one young player had been reprimanded for joyfully throwing his cap high in the air at Lord's after taking a boundary catch dismissing a troublesome Middlesex batsman. Now such enthusiasm was not to be stifled but charted and controlled; in all, there was much to be pleased about in Lancashire cricket in 1965 – if you look deep enough!

It was the same in 1966. Statham and his side moved up the championship table just one rung and the returns of some of the more experienced players were far from impressive. Yet the new captain was creating team spirit and encouraging new men. Green was the only batsman to top the thousand run mark but Pullar, Bond, Knox and Worsley all batted soundly at times and Lloyd, a young Accrington left-hander, came on to the scene to show considerable promise. Statham remained the bulkhead and the spearhead although he was reaching the stage in life when fast bowling called for tremendous physical effort. Higgs was not quite in gear but Lever bowled better than ever and Shuttleworth showed signs of having what it takes to make the grade. Pilling and Sullivan made little progress, but these were early days for two raw recruits and Lancashire saw in Goodwin, another Central Lancashire League recruit, the makings of a very capable wicketkeeper.

Also on the scene for the first time was a young Yorkshire-born all rounder by the name of Wood. He had been sent across the Pennines by Yorkshire chairman Brian Sellars with the message: 'Give him a chance, he can do you a lot of good.' Wood took time to settle in but in due course he fulfilled all that was foreshadowed.

What Statham really lacked was a good off-spinner to supplement the efforts of Greenhough, and in a summer of many responsive pitches it was this 'missing link' that retarded any rapid progress from a happy side now establishing much better relationship with both committee and members. These are factors not to be ignored. The impatient ones among the members, however, were still far from happy in 1967 when

Lancashire, under Statham, again only won four championship games against three lost and seventeen drawn, to move up to the eleventh spot in the table.

The introduction of Atkinson from Somerset as an opening batsman of experience proved a wise signing. The new man, Yorkshire-born, rivalled Pilling as the side's most consistent scorer. Both topped the thousand run mark, and although Pullar failed to reach that illustrious milestone and Green faded into insignificance, Wood and Lloyd more than made up the deficit. No bowler could claim a hundred wickets but Statham with eighty-nine victims and Higgs with seventy-four saw to it that the opposition usually had a fight on their hands. Shuttleworth advanced to capture forty-five victims and Lever was always doing useful work with a similar reward. Greenhough had gone, but Savage, a Lancashire-born veteran off-spinner from Leicestershire, returned home to lend variety to an attack by claiming fifty-four wickets at reasonable cost.

One unhappy memory of the season was the complete abandonment of two important Old Trafford games. Pullar's benefit match against Warwickshire on 20, 21 and 22 May was never started because of pouring rain, and a week later the roses clash against Yorkshire suffered a similar fate, with conditions so bad that the players never went to the ground. Saturday's play was abandoned on the Friday and with the rain continuing there was no cricket at headquarters for two weeks. Statham was invited to continue as captain in 1968 but, offered a business appointment to commence at the end of that summer, expressed a desire to stand down and play alongside a new captain. He promised all aid possible and Lancashire, still well aware of the need for strengthening and supporting the new rules for special registrations for a limited number of overseas players, appointed Bond to lead the side in succession to the ever-willing Statham. In addition, they secured the services of the highly talented and spectacular Indian wicketkeeper, Farokh Engineer, to bolster up the batting. The club also made a great effort to sign Gary Sobers but were out-bid by Nottinghamshire. Instead, they made arrangements with the Lancashire League club, Haslingden, to take the West Indies left-hander, Clive Lloyd, when his contract ended at the end of the 1968 season. It meant that Lloyd, one of the most attractive stroke players in the game and an outstanding fieldsman, could not play until the end of the West Indies half tour in 1969, but Lancashire were content to wait. In the meantime, Bond took over and at once impressed as a leader of rare ability.

Perhaps it was the fact that he had experienced failure on his own account and tolerated it more in others that made Bond an instant success. For success he was. Within weeks the side became a happy band of strolling players. They won only eight championship matches, drew fourteen and lost six in rising from the eleventh place to the sixth. At the same time more youngsters were blooded and given extended runs. Bailey came from Durham to brighten up the batting and set new fielding standards in the covers. For almost the first time it was plain to see the results of good and happy teamwork. Only Pilling topped the thousand run mark but Bond, top of the averages and always setting the right example, Lloyd (D.), Atkinson and Wood all batted soundly to make up for the sudden departure of Green to Gloucestershire at the height of his power.

Why allow a punishing batsman of Green's calibre to go? The answer was to be found in Bond's desire for teamwork as opposed to individualism, and when Pullar showed signs of dissatisfaction he, too, was allowed to join the west country club, as Lancashire boldly planned for the future with the accent on youth and the aid to come from Clive Lloyd.

Engineer had already settled in well. A punishing batsman, the Indian did not perhaps score as many runs as expected but his first season's return of 692 for an average of nearly seventeen was not to be ignored – especially as he also brought a completely new look to the wicketkeeping role. Flamboyant at times, but always sound, Engineer brought a touch of spectacular aggression to the rapidly improving scene. Higgs was top wicket-taker, with 105 victims, but Statham, happily edging out of the game, satisfied himself with sixty-seven and marked his final appearance against Yorkshire with one of his most hostile spells in the last hour of the opening day at Old Trafford. Cheered to the echo as he went in to bat, Statham expressed his appreciation by 'mowing down' the first five Yorkshire wickets for a mere twelve runs in a match set aside for Higgs' benefit. Statham so whet the appetite that when play reopened on the Sunday afternoon over twenty-one thousand crammed into Old Trafford to see if he could complete the demolition.

18. STATHAM GOES IN GLORY

Alas, he could not, although the most popular Lancashire bowler in years had final figures of 6-34 in a Yorkshire total of 61, he could not keep it up. With a stubborn 77 from Brian Close, Yorkshire saved the game, and the day; but the glory went, for the very last time, to Statham.

With Statham gone, Lancashire lost a little ground in the county championship in 1969, but they took to the new Sunday Competition sponsored by John Player & Co. with rare relish, and walked away with the title. At the same time they heralded a completely new look from the spectator point of view, and long before the new championship was won Old Trafford was housing exciting and enthusiastic hordes of over ten thousand to watch Bond and his men produce the new all-action cricket that guaranteed not only a result but also some cricketing fireworks in the course of the five-hour battle. The secret of the side's success lay with Bond's interpretation of the part the new league was to play. Like many other county cricketers, several of his men did not like sacrificing technical ideals for the sake of quick scoring. Nor did they relish the demand to hit out or get out that inevitably arose when victory was being pursued. But Bond took the common-sense view. He knew how much depended upon the crowd-pulling success of the new tournament. 'We may not really like it, but it can win back the crowds and find the money to finance the three-day game. Let's go out there and enjoy it. If we can get some fun out of it I am sure the crowds will,' said Bond. He was proved right, and Lancashire, still struggling to find their feet in the county championship sphere, were an instant success in the one-day game. Engineer and Clive Lloyd were, of course, tailor-made for this aggressive brand of the game but it did not take the majority of Bond's own men long to learn what it was all about. It meant hard hitting, accurate bowling and razor-keen fielding – and Lancashire supplied it.

Yet over the championship course they won only two matches, drew twenty-one and lost one. The weather often defied them and the state of the pitches, especially at Old Trafford where they were too slow to encourage either batsmen or bowlers, was an added obstacle that could not be overcome. Pilling and David Lloyd were the only batsmen to top the thousand run figure, though Engineer might have done so but for an injury towards the end of the campaign. Clive Lloyd, coming on the scene as a regular player at the end of the West Indies tour in mid-season, soon made his mark with 367 runs in thirteen innings, and Bailey batted consistently for over five hundred runs in seventeen matches. Bond contributed 660 runs but Wood could not win a regular place and Sullivan, too, was in and out. Higgs lost his appetite for the game and took only sixty-five wickets before announcing his retirement, soon after getting his benefit award, but Lever and Shuttleworth made up a steady pace combination and Hughes came along to provide left-hand spin and hard-hitting batsmanship in promising style. Simmons was recruited from professionalism at Blackpool to provide the off-spin when Savage found the going too hard, and all in all Lancashire were beginning to be talked about in cricketing circles stretching from Lord's to the village green.

The best was yet to come! In 1970 Lancashire not only won the John Player League for the second time but also added the Gillette Cup to their haul and finished third in the county championship to Kent and Glamorgan. Again Bond proved himself an inspired leader and with Wood, Hughes and Simmons settling down into top-class players the summer proved one of great delight. Ever ready to accept a challenge, and never loath to dangle a carrot in front of the opposition, Lancashire again romped away with the Sunday League. They also made light work of winning the Gillette Cup, for the first time beating Sussex with undisguised ease in the final at Lord's and generally leaving no real doubt about their superiority at over-limited cricket. As always Clive Lloyd proved a key figure, but Pilling could seldom be faulted and when called upon the so-called 'staider' batsmen like David Lloyd and Wood generally rose to the occasion. Lever and Shuttleworth settled down to become as consistent a pair of new ball bowlers as any in the country and each won England caps in the makeshift series against the Rest of the World as well as places in the MCC touring team to Australia and New Zealand.

It was another summer of big crowds and enthusiastic demonstrations. Bond became accepted as the leading disciple of the new-look cricket but he never forgot to pay tribute to his men or to encourage them to give of their best. His one complaint was that the weather and the state of the wickets offered him little scope in the serious business of three-day championship cricket. Old Trafford's pitches remained slow and unresponsive and it was more or less the same wherever the team played. Only six championship games were won against two lost and sixteen drawn; yet the team finished third in the final reckoning and but for a hurricane century by Walker, of Glamorgan, at Cardiff, might have just got the better of the Welsh side to finish second. Clive Lloyd, Pilling and Wood all topped the thousand run mark. David Lloyd was close on hand, whilst Bond and Engineer were seldom found wanting.

In addition, Lancashire found a highly promising newcomer in Hayes. Coming on to the staff from Sheffield University after playing with great effect at schools and at youth representative level, the young Marple batsman hit 682 runs in fifteen matches to create tremendous interest and win a place in England's under twenty-three team at Scarborough. Hayes started off with a bang. He narrowly failed to hit a century on his début against Middlesex and reached ninety-nine shortly afterwards against Hampshire before being dismissed going for a big hit in a chase against the clock. Hayes is not strictly speaking an orthodox batsman but he has a wide range of scoring strokes and is never afraid to employ them. Along with Snellgrove, he represented the younger school of Lancashire batsmen which Bond was gradually breaking in, and although there were signs that 'the big one got away' – a reference to the county title – Lancashire had firmly re-established themselves as trend-setters in the rapidly changing world of big cricket.

They had certainly come a long way since the doldrums of the centenary year, and although the John Player League title eluded Bond and his men in 1971 the team retained the Gillette Cup in a memorable final clash with Kent at Lord's and again finished third in the county championship. Once again there could be no denying the team's crowd-pulling power, and wherever they went, in all three branches of the game that now make up a summer calendar, Lancashire were regarded as the Manchester United of cricket. How strange both teams should live within a six hit of each other at Old Trafford.

Individual performances were on a similar par to 1970. The two Lloyds, Wood, Pilling and Snellgrove were the side's major batsmen. Lever, Shuttleworth, Hughes and Simmons provided the bowling ammunition, and in the field Clive Lloyd again led the keenest and most dynamic run-savers and catchers the game has seen in a long time. Bond's captaincy left no grounds for complaint. If the little Bolton man ever made a mistake it was quickly covered up by men eager to stress their loyalty to a captain extraordinary. Times without number, Lancashire confounded the opposition by accepting challenges to hit runs against the clock. Seldom did they come adrift under these circumstances, and rarely, when the boot was on the other foot, did Bond's bowlers fail to find the answer. There were men out of touch, as there always will be, and Pilling had to struggle more than usual for his four-figure tally of runs. Hayes lost form at the beginning of the season, and such was Lancashire's batting strength the Marple youngster could not get back, although gradually fighting his way to form again in the second team. When eventually Hayes did get another senior chance he found the demands of time-limit cricket a barrier to the playing of his normal game, but he cheerfully sacrificed himself for the sake of the team – no man can do more!

All in all, Lancashire have still some way to go before everybody at Old Trafford can be satisfied the battle has been won. What can be said without fear of contradiction is that Lancashire cricket is again respectable. In the course of the last twenty years it came perilously close to being the laughing stock of the sporting world. Club comedians were making jokes at their expense and even the league and club cricketers that abound in a closely knit cricketing community were prone to snigger at the mention of Lancashire and their misdeeds. The gulf between those who played and those who controlled grew so wide that many despaired of it ever being breached. That it took a rebellion to do it was a matter for much concern. That the ends justified the means cannot be denied. Lancashire cricket now vibrantly throbs with promise, enterprise and goodwill. The relationship between the county club and the rest of the cricketing world inside the county is better and happier than it has ever been before, though that problems will arise and differences of opinion occur is inevitable in an area where so many play the game at different levels.

What really matters is that Old Trafford now clearly illustrates all that is best in cricket. On the field Bond and his men are accepted as the game's top entertainers. Off it, with Chairman Cedric Rhoades, the live wire, the administrative set-up has become united and unifying. Help for the strugglers is always at hand; advice can always be obtained. Even cash for those in difficult straits can now be made available. Times have changed, and where there once was aloofness and even contempt for the rest of the county's cricketing clubs there is now sympathy, understanding, and an even greater desire to cooperate still further as cricket fights on against a modern world geared to space travel and mass entertainment at the turn of a knob.

The statistical story of how success was achieved and failure suffered on the field has now been told. What remains to be related is of the struggle behind the scenes. There is more to cricket than is to be seen on the field!

Part Three

The management and staff

19. WORKING BEHIND THE SCENES

It takes more than good players, more than the scoring of runs
and the capturing of wickets, to make a successful cricket club.
The team that represents Lancashire or any other county on the
field of play is only one part of a club. Behind the scenes there
must be men of courage, men of vision, and above all men
dedicated to the summer game and all it stands for. In the main
they are men of stature; men with influence; and men prepared
to give of their time and often their money to see that nothing
besmirches the good name of a game that has long been accepted
as a way of life – British life in particular!

In the beginning, the administration of Lancashire cricket was
on a voluntary basis, with a president, chairman, secretary and
treasurer representing the 'engine room'. Basically, things have
not changed in a hundred years or more. Old Trafford's figure-
heads are still the president, the chairman, the secretary and the
treasurer. It is the character and reputation of these key figures
that make the difference between a good club and a bad one, a
successful one or an unsuccessful one, and down the years
Lancashire cricket has been served well by the busy men behind
the scenes. Not for them the glamour and the glory, the fame
and often the fortune, that goes to the master batsman or the ace
bowler. Yet one could not survive without the other. There are
many who maintain that it is far more important to have a good
team off the field than it is to have a good one on it. That is,
perhaps, overstating the case, but one plain fact emerges. No
cricket club can be successful unless its administrators and its
players are happily married and living together in complete

112

harmony. Mutual trust, mingled with admiration for each other, is worth much more than a thousand runs or a hundred wickets a season from any player.

In the early days, when professionalism was on a part-time basis and matches were mainly played at home, finance was not of prime importance. There was no charge for admission to see Manchester or Lancashire play their earliest matches, and there was certainly no payment offered or demanded by the enthusiastic and hard-working officials like Mark Phillips, the first president, John Holt, the first treasurer, or Sydney H. Swire, a secretary beyond compare and a truly honorary one at that.

Strangely, and in a sense sadly, Lancashire's records do not list the names of the men who have accepted the difficult and frequently onerous role of committee chairman. To him has always fallen the duty of – to use a modern sporting phrase borrowed from another game – the link man. The chairman of a county cricket club is more than a mere head of the committee. He is the man in day-to-day touch with the secretary, and the person who must make and accept the responsibility for the snap decisions that must be so often made without reference to the committee – yet subject to their approval when the time comes. There have been times when the club president has been a real worker and not merely a figurehead. Choosing him carefully is therefore an essential part of cricket administration and in this capacity Lancashire's choice has covered a wide field.

Primarily the world of commerce has produced the man of the moment. Men like Phillips, Sir Edwin Stockton, Sir Edward Rhodes and Sir Stanley Holt were businessmen who commanded considerable influence and were prepared to use it in the interest of the club and its reputation. Peers of the realm like Lord Derby, Lord Ashton and Lord Stanley were also men who could speak and act for the club in the highest circles of the land. Men of the cloth, like the Reverend V. F. Royle, and the well beloved Canon Paton-Williams, guaranteed Lancashire cricket an eminence in hallowed as well as influential quarters, and it was not without intent that old players of the calibre of A. B. Rowley, A. N. Hornby, R. H. Spooner, R. A. Boddington and G. O.

H   113

Shelmerdine stepped from the field to the highest of the administrative offices with dignity and pride. They represented that blessed band without which cricket could not exist – men who enjoyed playing the game and then turned to administrating it as a token of appreciation for the pleasure they had obtained from it. In a nutshell, men who wanted to put something back into cricket.

Men with military bearing like Colonel Green added lustre to Lancashire cricket both on and off the field and the medical world provided two outstanding club officials in Dr H. H. J. Hitchen and Dr J. B. Holmes. Neither men were cricketers of outstanding merit, except at club level, but they gave to their county service that can be ranked with that of the most successful batsmen and bowlers. *Wisden*, alas, does not record such deeds, nor does any other publication. That they are of prime importance cannot be denied.

Only men of distinction are ever invited to occupy the top spot in Lancashire cricket and when, in 1971, Sir Neville Cardus was elected to the highest office his beloved county had to offer he confessed himself touched beyond all measure. That he should be considered a figurehead is incidental. There can be no doubt that he can provide a journalistic sphere of influence no cricketing body can afford to ignore. He, above all others, gave to Lancashire cricket and cricketers an immortality few other counties have or can command. In his term of office he will, undoubtedly, do much to enhance and sustain the happy relationship now existing between the club and the press. It has not always been so.

Another pleasing feature of Lancashire administration is that many of the club presidents 'worked' for their promotion. Sir Edwin Stockton and R. A. Boddington each served long terms as honorary treasurers, the men with their hands on the purse strings, and others were committee members of long standing before they were elected to the highest office. And there is nothing in club records to even hint at opposition to any name ever put forward as president of the Lancashire County Cricket Club. Bickering there may well have been behind the scenes – and that is not to be regarded as a sign of weakness – but always at annual meetings there has been unanimous and enthusiastic support for the man nominated. That is as it should be, and it speaks well for Lancashire's cricketing traditions that few annual meetings have been stormy ones.

Inevitably on occasions there has been criticism and censure. Once there was certainly upheaval but no club passing its centenary year can expect to sail for ever on smooth seas. In point of fact it took an upheaval, not so many years ago, to stop the ship drifting on to the rocks. Even at the expense of some mud-slinging and some departures, order brought out of chaos often strengthens a cause.

Well blessed by its presidents and well served by its treasurers, Lancashire cricket has also much to be thankful for in its choice and utilisation of secretaries. None deserves more praise than the first of the six who have held office from 1873 to 1972. Sydney H. Swire was that rare cricketing species, a hard-working unpaid secretary who officially took over in 1873 and remained in charge until 1906, when he stepped aside happy in the knowledge that he had helped establish the club on a solid foundation. Mr Swire had been one of the prime movers in the founding of the club in 1864 and although not generally acknowledged as the club secretary until nine years later it was obvious that he had been acting in that capacity from the very beginning. His contribution cannot be overestimated. He had played the game in his youth and stayed on to set the example of putting something back into it and that has always been the basis of every successful cricket club. To Mr Swire must go the credit for the initial hard work that saw Manchester cricket become Lancashire cricket and an amateur club develop into a highly successful and well respected professional one.

In his day Swire kept the peace between many temperamental players and stubborn committee members. The great Sydney Barnes, generally admitted to be one of the most difficult of playing characters, was once heard to say, 'If there were more like Mr Swire and Mr MacLaren in the game there would be better players and better cricket.' Be that as it may, S. H. Swire saw to it that Lancashire cricket was administered with dedicated zeal and an understanding of the needs of all. When Mr Swire stepped down, T. J. Matthews stepped up and was in control from 1906 until 1921. His were the days of many changes and, of course, the first long interruption of play during the first world war. Like his predecessor, Mr Matthews earned a reputation for being approachable and fair in his dealings both with players and members. That he was a busy man goes without saying for his years in office were ones of immense growth.

Matthews saw the first-class game expand from occasional matches to a full-time occupation. The one-day games were overhauled by the two-day and eventually the three-day matches, and the county championship programme developed into cricket on six days of almost every week. At the same time, membership grew and finance became important. The more cricket that was played, the more the players required. Even with outstanding amateur support Lancashire were always in need of professional assistance, and soon the paid players began to outnumber the unpaid ones in the services of the club. A man of great energy and great tact, Mr Matthews saw to it that good cricket was harnessed to first-class administration and was well esteemed by all in the cricketing world. In 1921 he handed over to H. Rylance, and Lancashire cricket was again in safe hands. Harry Rylance was to serve the club nobly and well for eleven years, and during that time Lancashire gained more honours than most. His term of office was not without incident. Famous players caused temporary and temperamental embarrassment but always the good of the club was put before the whims of the individual and Lancashire remained a successful and highly respected cricketing combination.

20. TIMES OF STRESS

At loggerheads at times with other clubs over incidents on the field, the county remained dignified if defiant, and in the course of time agreed to forgive and forget and get on with the playing of the game. There is no disgrace in the occasional disagreement and no point in existing if not prepared to fight for ideals. Battles on the field and off it were won and lost with equal respect and toleration of tactics.

When in 1932 Harry Rylance stepped down, his place was taken by Captain Rupert Howard, a man who had played an occasional game for the county as an amateur batsman of style and promise but who found that his real strength lay in the administrative field. A military man, Captain Howard set a high standard in both the quality of his work and the manner in which he controlled his staff at both office and playing level. He saw membership grow and crowd support increase and slump. He watched established players fade and new ones make the grade. Under his control was a playing staff at its biggest and a programme of cricket ranging from the club and ground matches undertaken by the Manchester club to the minor county and first-class programme – and it made for a busy life. Captain Howard became not only a highly successful and popular secretary of Lancashire but also an acknowledged leader in his own field and was the first Old Trafford official to be asked to manage an MCC tour to Australia, when in the winter of 1936-7 he took charge of the side led by G. O. Allen. In so doing he established his reputation at international level, and after working feverishly in his spare time throughout the years of the second world war, when he was promoted to the rank of major, he was again honoured with the managership of W. R. Hammond's team Down Under in the winter of 1946-7. Major Howard thus bridged two cricketing decades and his success at international level did not blind him to his responsibilities at Lancashire heights. He, perhaps more than any other secretary before or after, inaugurated and maintained an agreeable measure of cooperation and coordination between the county club and the numerous smaller clubs in the leagues and associations that abound in the shire.

In a scattered and widely diversified cricketing community the relationship between county and league cricket can be a tricky business. The major leagues, rightly or wrongly, believe that they have a place in the cricketing scheme of things to be. Few will deny them that right. Yet they also have a duty to fit into the overall plan of cricket in the county, and in keeping a degree of mutual respect and cooperation between two highly competitive spheres Major Howard achieved much. He saw to it that the league clubs seldom appealed to Old Trafford for help that was not forthcoming and almost every Saturday a member of the Lancashire groundstaff could be seen helping out in the leagues if a club professional fell ill, was injured, or was required by his county. In return, the league concentrated on finding and encouraging young players to strive for a chance with the county and places on the groundstaff. It was not Major Howard's fault that when a young cricketer reached a standard which made him of interest to Old Trafford he often became lost to the leagues. He pleaded for a greater degree of tolerance and a widening of the rigid league rules that denied many a young professional a return to his home club when not required by the county. Such a state of affairs now exists and before he died Major Howard saw the beginning of a new deal bringing the leagues and the county much closer together. When he decided to leave cricket and concentrate on the demands of the family business in 1949 the major was succeeded by another Howard. G. C. Howard, no relation, a southerner who had been assistant secretary to the Surrey club at the Oval, was appointed his successor.

When Geoffrey Howard arrived on the scene, Lancashire were in the throes of rebuilding. There were playing problems galore. The captaincy was always a thorny problem. Professional players came and went with remarkable inconsistency. Good amateurs were few and far between. The standard of play suffered and so did the size of the club membership. Crowd support dwindled and the relationship between players and committee deteriorated until there was a marked lack of team spirit and understanding between the two spheres. There can be no clearer illustration of this than the perfectly true story of a long-serving committee man, talking to a member on the pavilion side before play began one morning, who heard and saw his colleague say 'Good morning' to a passer-by. 'I know that face. Who is he?' asked the committee member. The passer-by was Pullar, an England batsman as well as a Lancashire player and a member of the Old Trafford staff for several years – yet he was not recognised by a club official in a key position!

No man in his right senses could lay the blame entirely at the secretary's feet, and there can be no denying that Mr Howard did a great deal of good work for Lancashire and for England. Like his predecessor, he managed an MCC team in Australia and New Zealand and another in India and Pakistan. Yet it is true to say that he never really got to grips with the problems that abounded in Lancashire cricket at the time. As a southerner he could not be expected to understand the complicated position of the leagues. His job was to administer Lancashire cricket and to him that meant Old Trafford and the county game. What went on outside headquarters was, apparently, of little concern to him. Yet it was of vital importance, and the relationship between county club and the hundreds of league clubs suffered in consequence.

There was never open warfare; but neither was there full co-operation, and whilst it would be grossly unfair to saddle Mr Howard with the full responsibility for an unhappy situation this was the era when many good players from the leagues bypassed Old Trafford to make their name elsewhere. Frank Tyson was one. Keith Andrew was another. Both these England and Northamptonshire cricketers learned the game within a few miles of Old Trafford and actually had trials at the Lancashire nets. Yet they were allowed to migrate – and they were not the only ones. Something was lacking at Old Trafford and it was difficult to pinpoint the reason. There were many who considered the secretary lacked the right kind of advice and example from his committee but he had, at that time, a chairman who worked hard to present a united front in Lancashire cricket.

One of the major problems undoubtedly lay in the power held by the club's vice-presidents. In the main they consisted of old committee members, men honoured for their services in various walks of cricket life in the county. They were, in effect, the aldermanic bench on the council of the club and they were entitled to vote at committee meetings without having a thorough knowledge or understanding of decision taken by various sub-committees. It was an unwieldy and unsatisfactory form of government, and it undoubtedly did not help the secretary either in the discharge of his duties or in his relationship with the members and the public. There came into being a belief that

Lancashire

Lancashire County Cricket Club was a private organization beholden to none but its members and answerable only to them. That was all right in theory. But the club was accepting public responsibility for a county cricketing side and charging admission money to watch them. No wonder the popular side spectator was often irritated by an apparent lack of communication and even more hurtful display of unconcernedness at the way things were going on the field. It was not the secretary's fault and he was, without a shadow of doubt, very much concerned about a position rapidly bringing Lancashire cricket into disrepute. In the leagues there were sniggers at the county's lack of success. Part-time cricketers openly scoffed at the efforts of their so-called superiors and on the stage at many a working-man's club comedians were poking fun. What was worse was an apparent lack of concern about this in committee at Old Trafford.

Too much was being left to too few and Lancashire cricket was at its lowest ebb. Did nobody care? It became apparent in 1964, the club's centenary year, that somebody did and the pavilion side was rife with rumour and speculation about impending changes. Good young players were mysteriously dismissed and the captaincy was hawked around in a shameful and undignified manner. A year that should have been one for notable rejoicing turned out to be one of grave discontent, and it ended with an uprising. It also coincided with the decision of Secretary Howard to return to the Oval and take charge of his native Surrey.

Before the story of the upheaval can be unfolded it is necessary to enlarge upon the activities of the men who held the chairmanship at one time or another, and in this respect no name was more important than that of T. A. Higson. A remarkable little man was this Manchester city councillor, a solicitor by profession and an ardent cricket lover by inclination. Mr Higson played five matches for Lancashire between 1905 and 1923 but made little impression. Not for the first time, a modest player switched to the administration side and became a power in the land. First as a committee member, then as the club's honorary treasurer, and finally as committee chairman for a long spell, Mr Higson became a veritable cricketing dictator at Old Trafford. Small in

120

Above, Geoff Pullar, the only Lancashire batsman to hit a test century for England at Old Trafford

Peter Lever, a Lancashire bowler of test match status

Above, Frank Hayes,
a young batsman rich
in promise

Barry Wood,
recruited from
Yorkshire, is another
young player with
much to offer

Above, Clive Lloyd; a
bowler's view of
Lancashire's big-hitting
West Indies batsman

David Hughes, a young all-
rounder of great potential

Left, J. D. Bond, Lancashire's present captain and a man who has done much to revive a fading Red Rose side

A vital wicket falls. Clive Lloyd runs out Gloucestershire batsman David Green in the semi-final of the 1971 Gillette Cup at Old Trafford. Over 25,000 watched the game, which went on until nearly 9 pm

stature but immense in importance he ruled the club with an iron hand. Players were openly mistrustful and even frightened of him. Fellow officials respected him but seldom opposed his wishes. He was a man of tremendous energy and an iron will. He served England as a test selector and was listened to with respect at Lord's. No man could doubt his sincerity.

Higson wanted Lancashire to lead the way at cricket, and he was not prepared to be sidetracked in his efforts to get them to the top. A clever brain and an instinct for sizing up men and matters rapidly was accompanied by an uncanny ability to control a meeting and get his own way. He frequently ruled members out of order when they touched on controversial matters at annual meetings and seldom lost a chance to assert his authority over all and sundry. Always a busy little man, Mr Higson sincerely believed that it was his lot to signpost the way for Lancashire cricket. He was first elected chairman in 1932 but was at the zenith of his power immediately after the second world war. It was his keen brain that saw the necessity for rebuilding Old Trafford and it was his foresight that called for the establishment of a rebuilding fund. He set a target of £200,000 but never reached it. Yet donations flowed in from every part of the cricketing world, and although there were restrictions and difficulties all around there was no delay in re-establishing the Lancashire ground as one of the best in the world. The chairman was unable to find the money himself but he used his considerable influence to see it was raised, and when it came to hand he was again extremely active in finding ways and means, to say nothing of men and firms, who could get to work on the mammoth rebuilding task. Old Trafford today is a memorial to the thoroughness with which a zealous little man overcame all problems. From the administration point of view he steered Lancashire through crises that developed on the field and off. He earned the reputation of being a hard man and made many enemies by his refusal to tolerate opposition. He was never averse to issuing instructions calling for action on the field as well as off it.

Higson was likened by many to a non-playing captain as well as a chairman of committee and he dismissed public criticism as of no account whatsoever. Likewise he ignored it to concentrate on his own ideals and objectives for the betterment of Lancashire cricket. He took decisions, issued instructions, and answered for them when called upon to do so in the committee room. He had a persuasive tongue and a masterly way of making his committee see things his way. When all other means failed there were always the vice-presidents to rally to his support and seldom did the club 'aldermen' fail to give him the support he needed. It was no suprise, for it was frequently said that he proposed the election of the majority of them himself! He advocated two-day cricket for a time but quickly realized the weakness of his case and switched his thoughts and actions accordingly. He treated professional players as an employer treats employees and seldom mixed with them. On one notable occasion he was living in Manchester's leading hotel when Washbrook was presented with his record benefit cheque of £14,000, but he did not attend the dinner. He pleaded 'pressure of business' and ignored some pointed remarks that he was unwilling to witness one man handed so much money for simply doing a professional job of work.

Without a doubt, T. A. Higson was a pillar of strength to Lancashire cricket. No doubt his sole object was to enhance the club's reputation and sustain its responsibility. Undeniably no man worked harder, or longer, in a bid to keep his beloved club to the forefront. At the same time, his manner and his methods of working were hardly democratic ones. He died in 1949, before he could assume the highest honour of all, that of club president. Yet he left behind a reputation of service and dedication un-paralleled in Lancashire's cricketing history. That he made enemies as well as friends was inevitable. He was the kind of man who could not serve without leading, and the times he failed were far outnumbered by the times he succeeded. The part he played was a notable one, even a distinguished one, and he will never be forgotten – by friend or foe alike!

Dr J. B. Holmes held the chairmanship for a brief time after the death of Mr Higson, whom he had served under without complaint for many years, but it was when Mr T. E. Burrows took over that Lancashire began to realize the errors of their ways. Tommy Burrows never played first-class cricket. He enjoyed himself at club level but found his real niche on the administration side. It took him several years to reach committee status and one of the achievements that finally helped him to gain a place at Old Trafford was the magnificent way he organized the Washbrook benefit fund. A livewire and a tireless worker, Mr Burrows led the way in a new approach to cricketers' benefits. He saw the necessity for seeking new means and methods of support to augment the allocation of gate receipts set aside for a beneficiary in one match specially allocated. Often, after expenses had been paid, the reward was modest even if thankfully received. Under the inspiring example of Mr Burrows, and with the aid of an enthusiastic committee, Washbrook was to change all that. The secret was 'outside efforts'. They ranged from Sunday matches to raffles, from whip-rounds at work to collections round the ring, and again Lancashire led the way in the organisation of a cricketing new look.

Stepping up into the chair, Tommy Burrows, like T. A. Higson before him, spared nothing in an attempt to restore Lancashire's cricketing reputation. His methods and his demeanour were in complete contrast to those of Mr Higson. He made it his objective to get around the many leagues and clubs that make up the cricketing community in the county. For almost the first time Old Trafford acknowledged it was not the be all and end all of cricket in Lancashire. Tommy Burrows wooed the leagues and their clubs back into the fold. Mr Higson hardly knew they existed, and did not appear to concern himself much with their welfare, except in his own intimate sphere of the North Lancashire League where he donated a cup for competition and made an annual pilgrimage to present it.

Mr Burrows, on the other hand, lost no opportunity to visit either clubs or leagues. He saw their problems and acknowledged their part in the scheme of things. If they wanted help he tried to organize it. It was he who hit upon the happy idea of donating a small sum of money to each club who sent a recruit to make the grade at Old Trafford. It was a small gesture but a well received one and it made the league clubs feel that they had a part to play. Never too busy to spare the time and never too tired to make a journey, the Lancashire chairman did much to draw the so-called smaller cricketing fry back into the fold. He also took the leading part in the formation of the Lancashire Youth Cricket Council and accepted office with many other subsidiary cricketing bodies.

Unfortunately, Mr Burrows could not stop the rot on the field or encourage the members of his committee to move with the times. Unlike Mr Higson, Mr Burrows obeyed instructions instead of issuing them, and with many of his committee out of touch with a progressive cricketing age, Lancashire cricket drifted on to the rocks in its centenary year. The form of the team was poor. The spirit in which they played the game also lacked appeal, and one began to wonder if anybody really cared. Many members voiced their dissatisfaction. Most of them held forth on the pavilion side and in the bar. A few lodged complaints with the secretary. Others took the extreme step of resigning and staying away. Things were undoubtedly bad. The drift continued until a young Manchester textile merchant stepped in to draft a petition of protest and demand a special meeting to clear the air. His name was Cedric S. Rhoades, and he had not played the game except at minor league level. His experience of administration was limited to serving as his club honorary secretary and as a committee member. But he loved cricket, and it was distasteful as well as disastrous to him to see Lancashire cricket in a decline. He had supported the team at home and away for several years, and eventually he took action to stop the rot and usher in a new era. By the end of the 1964 season he had secured enough support to fulfil the club rules and demand a special general meeting. His petition was received with dismay, and efforts were made to try and talk him out of such drastic action. But Mr Rhoades was adamant. He had started the fight and he was determined to see it through.

21. NO CONFIDENCE VOTE

There was no drawing back. The petition had to be accepted and a meeting arranged. A vote of no confidence in the committee was drawn up and the stage cleared for action. It was inevitable that much dirty linen had to be washed in public but that was a small price to pay if Lancashire cricket was to redeem itself. In September 1964, with Geoffrey Howard resigning as secretary and J. B. Wood, a Yorkshireman from the world of Rugby League, appointed to succeed him, the meeting was held and the vote of no confidence carried by an overwhelming majority. Hard things were said. Serious charges were made and answered. Bitterness was evident and excuses not tolerated. In the end the members of the committee, sitting back to lick their wounds, decided to resign *en bloc*, but, with one or two exceptions, offer themselves for re-election at the annual meeting to follow towards the end of the year. Chairman Burrows was one of those who decided to fight back, but he resigned the chairmanship and when a new committee was finally elected it contained six of the old administrative members and six new ones.

What is more important, the annual meeting carried an alteration to rule depriving vice-presidents of the power of vote and veto and denying them the right to attend committee meetings. This step was essential if the new regime was to succeed, but the older members of the committee fought hard to retain their rights. In the end they over-reached themselves by appointing George Duckworth, the club's old England wicket keeper and a member of the committee at the time of the crash, to speak against the motion. It was a mistake. Duckworth described the vice-presidents as the amateurs and gentlemen of the club, essential to the well-being of it on and off the field. In view of the situation it was entirely the wrong path to take. It was the mismanagement of a committee dominated by vice-presidents that had brought about the slump and the crisis. Instead of winning support, Duckworth lost it, and the motion was carried. It cleared the way for a democratic approach, and with Rhoades, the most successful of the new candidates, accompanied by younger men, the new committee settled down to prepare the new deal.

First of all, they had to live down the misdeeds of their predecessors, who had antagonized the members still more by advertising for a new captain in the old-world columns of *The Times*. How many applied and of what quality they were, was never revealed, but certainly there was a reawakening of public support and goodwill when Statham was duly elected. The chairman of the new-look committee was T. A. Higson, son of the oldtime warrior, and a player and committee member for a number of years. He lacked his father's dominant personality but was a willing worker for the club cause. He was also a member of the legal profession and he led the committee quietly and efficiently.

There was general agreement that the road back was to be a hard one and a long one. One or two new members of the committee fell by the wayside through lack of patience or willingness to accept the majority view. But in the main the old mingled with the new reasonably well, and with Jack Wood settling in as a courteous and extremely efficient secretary the restoration period started on a harmonious note.

Several old problems remained – and quite a lot of new ones arose. Finance was the major talking point. Membership had slumped and so, of course, had the guaranteed income. The players wanted more money and greater security. The game demanded a more vigorous look and a more businesslike approach. Cricket had never been self-supporting. It had lived on patronage and membership with the help of gate receipts, and in an era with a far different economic climate these three sources of income were unreliable and unrealistic. Lancashire, like all other counties, had to look around for alternative means of income. Plans had been drawn up for the use of the Old Trafford pavilion as a winter social centre and these were put into operation. But this was merely scratching at the surface of a very deep-rooted problem.

More substantial and quicker means of making money had to be devised. Old Trafford with all its amenities cost a terrific amount to maintain and the days when it could lie idle seven months in the year were coming to an end. With great foresight, the new committee conceived a plan to utilize parts of the ground, not used for the playing of cricket, for building purposes. There was a great demand for out-of-town business premises at the time and Lancashire decided to cash in on this demand. A plan was drawn up for a three-stage building scheme that would relieve the club of a tremendous financial burden. It called for the erection of towering blocks of offices behind the pavilion, along-side the practice ground already used as a car park. It meant considerable inconvenience to members and public alike but there would be no interference with the playing facilities or amenities. Artistically approached and tactfully introduced, it was estimated that the plan could, on fruition, bring in more than £50,000 a year in ground rents and fringe revenue.

The committee backed the scheme wholeheartedly but it had to be 'sold' to the members, and opposition could be anticipated. A scale model was drawn up and press aid recruited to help launch the new plan. On paper it looked dignified and blended well into Old Trafford's historic surroundings, but it obviously reduced amenities especially from the points of view of approach and car parking comfort. It was here that Cedric Rhoades stepped in. He was elected to propose the adoption of the scheme at the next annual meeting; it was the acid test for the new-comer, often wrongly tagged a 'rebel', from the administration point of view. The members were circularized with full details and given a promise that it would not be carried out without their approval. Its drawbacks were admitted but its good points equally stressed. Overall lay the undoubted financial gain it would provide. Criticism was rife.

The elderly members of the club regarded the scheme as an affront to their privacy and comfort. Many were prepared and even offered to pay more for the privilege of membership to keep Old Trafford's old look and reputation. They meant well but had not realized the full extent of the need for bigger and guaranteed financial stability. Before the meeting the scale model was on view in the pavilion Long Room and Mr Rhoades was on hand to explain the need for its implementation and the necessity for its introduction as soon as possible. He admitted the snags but could see no other way of preserving the ground for cricket. He declared a respect for tradition but proclaimed a greater desire to plan for the future. The scheme was still in the balance when he rose to put the motion to the meeting. It was not perhaps his first public speech but it was an historic and memorable one. He pleaded, almost begged, the members to accept the inevitable. Cricket under the shadow of big buildings was better than no

127

cricket at all, was his theme. He stressed the delicacy with which the architects had planned to merge the old with the new, and stressed that certain rights, especially with regard to car parking, had been reserved. But his trump card was a promise that the proposed three-phase plan would be reviewed at the end of each separate phase and the members consulted again. He carried the day and a decision as important as any ever taken at Old Trafford cleared the way for a complete revision of cricket and its modern requirements from both the playing and the financing points of view.

Back in committee it was now possible to turn attention to the demands of the players and the need for drawing up a new playing charter. If cricket was to live alongside more progressive sports, in face of mass entertainment brought into the home, old ideals and ideas had to be abandoned. Lancashire boldly supported the introduction of cup cricket, accepted the necessity for sponsorship, and led the demand for the introduction of talented overseas players into the first-class game at county championship level. They were united in their resolve that the future of Lancashire cricket inevitably depended upon the discovery and training of their own native-born recruits via the leagues and their associated clubs. But they considered it necessary to sign on one or two players of ability and crowd-pulling potential in order to give them more time to find and encourage their own boys.

Confident of the success of their proposal, overtures were made to the one man who possessed the necessary qualifications to provide sparkle on the field. Gary Sobers was their target. Ironically, the county could have had Sobers and a host of other world-class players in their ranks years before, when the various Lancashire leagues abounded with the best cricketers the world had ever produced. The late Sir Frank Worrell played with Radcliffe before Sobers did and would have migrated willingly to Lancashire and Old Trafford had the then club committee not stubbornly refused to 'trade' with league clubs. In the Lancashire and Central Lancashire leagues they could have taken their pick from Australia as represented by Ray Lindwall (Nelson), Bruce Dooland (East Lancashire), George Tribe (Rawtenstall) and Bill Alley (Colne). From the West Indies, Everton Weekes (Bacup),

Clyde Walcott (Enfield) and the great Learie Constantine (Nelson) had all been on offer. South Africa could have contributed Hugh Tayfield (East Lancashire) and India offered Vinoo Mankad (Haslingden), Vijay Hazare (Royton) and fast bowling Dhatu Phadkar (Rochdale). New Zealand sent John Reid over to Heywood, and all, almost without exception, would have jumped at the chance to play for Lancashire.

Yet other counties were allowed to nip in and profit from the enterprise of the small but ambitious league clubs, all within a fifty-mile radius of Old Trafford. It was said that Lancashire had given Lord's an assurance that they would not capitalize on the availability of these talented players. One wonders why? All could have been signed at nominal cost and introduced after short qualification periods. When the step was taken and international players granted the right of entry into first-class cricket in general, and Lancashire cricket in particular, it opened the possibility of a costly 'auction' and a free-for-all skirmish for the best players, with money the bargaining factor and long-term contracts the bugbear.

Nottinghamshire outbid Lancashire for Sobers but the club signed Farokh Engineer (India) and Clive Lloyd (West Indies) at less cost and with far greater potential. Both were introduced without embarrassment and at considerable gain from the team spirit and crowd-pulling view-points. Lancashire also played their full part in the introduction of Sunday cricket and the John Player League. The days when they went to Lord's to listen and support had gone. Now, with Cedric Rhoades as a live-wire chairman, Lancashire are listened to with respect and even admiration. Rhoades has teamed up with Secretary Jack Wood to lead an administrative team happy at their work and united in their resolve to play a full part in the cricketing shape of things to come.

When it became obvious that the first phase of the rebuilding plan had achieved far more than expected from the financial standpoint it was possible not only to consider and implement a new deal for the players, with increased salary scales and long-term contracts, but also to sell the ground rents and invest the better part of £100,000 at a rate of income better than usual

I

without the risk of responsibility for future repairs or tenancy.

All in all, the rebuilding scheme achieved much in its first phase. So much so, in point of fact, that the second and third phases have been abandoned and finance is no longer a major problem at Old Trafford. Quite apart from his relationship with the secretary, a charming man and unquestionably an ideal official, Cedric Rhoades has developed an understanding with the captain and the players which makes Lancashire the envy of the rest of the English cricketing world. Where once there was apathy, dismay and even disgust, there is now sincere regard, a lively cooperation, and the happiest possible team spirit. With Bond on the field and Rhoades off it, Lancashire have struck the ideal combination for success. Bond has earned the respect and admiration of his players; Rhoades has won the support and backing of his committee and members. The good effects are obvious. In 1970 and 1971 Lancashire won major cricketing honours in the new one-day sphere. It is true that the county championship still eludes them but there is ample evidence in the continued good spirit of the side and the gradual introduction of new players that the big prize is within reach. As an important bonus comes a much closer relationship and liaison with the many leagues and associations inside the county. Chairman Rhoades has been around and about to great effect and Captain Bond has lent full support. A united team and a unified committee will still have to face problems and iron out snags. That is cricket. The main source of satisfaction comes from the knowledge that membership is booming and that crowd support is the envy of all other cricketing counties; Old Trafford is no longer one of the most publicized ghost-spots in sport.

22. THEY ALSO SERVE

In paying tribute to the men behind the scenes in Lancashire cricket the groundsmen must not be overlooked. Upon them, down the years, has fallen the task of preparing the pitches and generally attending to all the jobs so vitally necessary to earn and maintain Old Trafford's reputation of being one of the best cricketing venues in the world. Players from every cricketing country have paid tribute to the conditions under which they are invited to 'work' at the Lancashire headquarters. There have been times when the bowlers have grumbled and times when the batsmen have been far from happy, but there can be no denying that to play in a test match at Old Trafford is to savour cricketing conditions at their very best. Today the Lancashire ground is one of the few major cricketing venues that still provide a sight screen at each end. No doubt the fact the pitch is broadside to the pavilion helps the authorities to maintain tradition and give the batsmen a perfect sight of the ball. There are occasions, of course, when spectators move behind the bowler's arm but there are less of these interruptions at Old Trafford than elsewhere in big cricket, and there can be no overestimating the good work accomplished by the club groundsmen. There are not very many of them and no records have been kept to provide the full list but five of them are worthy of mention.

First came Fred Reynolds, one of the old brigade of professional cricketers who numbered groundsmanship among his arts. The taking of wickets and the scoring of runs was never quite enough for old Fred, and he often boasted of his ability to produce pitches that gave batsmen and bowlers a fair chance of success. 'Mind ye,' said Reynolds on one occasion when complimented on the production of a good cricketing wicket, 'a man has to work for his wickets and for his runs too, but who wants or gets reward without sweating a bit?' Such was the Reynolds's theory, and he put it into practice. His were the days, at the turn of the century, when the tools for the job were primitive and his staff just one boy and a horse to pull both the roller and the cutter. Nowadays the modern groundsman has a fleet of expensive and complicated machines to help him prepare the pitch for action; yet in the leisurely days when Reynolds was preparing Old Trafford not only for first-class but also for club matches he managed to produce pitches that not only looked well but played well. And in his spare time he was never averse to tending to the wants of thirsty members in the pavilion bar.

Likewise, Reynolds's wife saw to it that Old Trafford was

always spick and span. The pavilion was her domain. The field belonged to her husband and between them they served the cause of Lancashire cricket with rare enthusiasm and much hard labour. In terms of cash their reward was small but living accommodation was also provided and Fred was seldom heard to bemoan his lot. He was a craftsman, on the field and off it, and he set a standard which only the best have been able to maintain.

Tom Matthews followed in the footsteps of Reynolds. He, too, was a man with a tremendous appetite for cricket, and with the help of one horse and one teenage assistant he never failed to make Old Trafford into one of the best cricket grounds in the country – nay, in the the world! Matthews confessed to having a hasty temper and being a bit 'testy', and it is recorded that on one occasion before the first world war he upset some of cricket's top brass by loudly ordering them to keep off the grass which he was lovingly preparing for a vital game. Unknown to Matthews he had addressed his remarks, unparliamentary but easy to understand, to some visitors from Lord's and he had to go, cap in hand, and humbly apologize for his behaviour before the committee of the day regarded the incident as closed. Even then, it is said, Tom scored well with his parting shot at the visiting gentry. 'If they come fra Lord's they should ah known better,' were his words as he left the secretary's office, duly admonished but obviously far from repentant. Matthews, like Reynolds, was never averse to filling in some of his spare time as the club barman, and it was often his proud boast that he worked from sun-up to sun-down on the field and then attended to the wants of thirsty members until the law demanded the bar be closed. A full life, and, no doubt, a satisfying one.

Arthur Widdowson was probably the first Lancashire groundsman to 'mechanize' the job of ground preparation, and he earned a reputation not only for the perfect state of the Old Trafford pitch but also for the velvety appearance of the outfield. The bowlers in Widdowson's day were often heard to proclaim that the groundsman was no friend to them. Widdowson, it appears, placed great faith in a special kind of marl, then readily available, and it was this substance which enabled him to prepare the perfect batting wickets Lancashire so proudly boasted in the late

1920s and the early 1930s. Widdowson, rightly or wrongly, earned the reputation of being a perfectionist, and it is said that he could often be seen in the outfield on his hands and knees uprooting the occasional daisy roots which he considered not only a blemish to Old Trafford but also an affront to his professional pride.

Certainly, both Cec. Parkin and Dick Tyldesley, long-suffering spinners in the days of Widdowson, once upset not only the groundsman but the entire ground staff by digging out large lumps of turf in their efforts to obtain a satisfactory foot-hold in one rain-affected match. Widdowson and his staff, looking on from their quarters with undisguised fury, were so angry that they walked in protest to the dressing room and then to the secretary's office to lodge an official complaint about the 'ruination of the square'. Not until the club committee had debated the matter at some length was the incident closed with a plea on the dressing room notice board to the effect that 'all players must observe the wishes of the groundstaff when securing firm footholds'. What Parkin and Tyldesley thought about things is certainly not recorded, more's the pity.

Harry Williams followed Widdowson, who took his highly developed arts and skills from Old Trafford to Trent Bridge where he built up an even greater reputation as the producer of perfect batting pitches. Williams, a little man who could seldom be seen without a dog at his heel or a county cap upon his head, not only produced the sort of cricketing pitches Lancashire demanded but also attended to the damage done when Hitler's invading Luftwaffe dropped a bomb slap bang in the middle of the test match pitch. Club officials were in a panic. A bomb crater some six feet deep, and scarred turf for yards around, presented a terrible sight, but Williams took one look and said, 'Ah well, I reckon A've got time to patch it up afore we play t'next test.' He had, and he did. When in 1945 Old Trafford staged a victory test between England and the Australian Services Elevens, playing conditions were as perfect as ever – and it was certainly not Harry Williams's fault that there still remained traces of bomb damage and wartime misusage around the ring and in the stands. When the game returned to normal, Harry, with his dog at his heels, his county cap worn at a jaunty angle, and his broomstick slung across his shoulder, became as well-known as any in the game. And what do you think was the name he gave to his faithful hound? None other than 'Trafford'. There were times when the players and the critics found fault with the state of the pitch but Williams rode the storms.

And so did Bert Flack who followed him and is still in command today. A real man of the soil, Flack learned his job at Fenner's, and he brought from his native Cambridgeshire not only an ability to prepare first-class pitches but a desire to live up to the reputation of his several illustrious predecessors. He has not failed. Today Bert Flack is the Harry Wheatcroft of groundsmen. His whiskers and his rosy complexion typify the man who not only tends the soil at Old Trafford but also pushes back the flood waters. Rain and cricket at Old Trafford are synonymous in many minds. Yet no groundsman ever worked harder than Flack to master not only the arts of preparing pitches but also of rescuing them from the floods that so frequently descend to make his life a nightmare. It may well be true that Flack has at his command the very best machinery it is possible to purchase in the realms of groundsmanship. What is equally true is that none but Flack could use them to such magnificent effect. Like the RAF in wartime, Flack can do the difficult in a matter of minutes. The extraordinary can be accomplished in half an hour, but he needs at least an hour to perform a miracle! He has proved it time without number in his days at Old Trafford. With the air of a man resigned to hard labour, Flack and his staff will survey the watery wastes that so often present themselves at the Lancashire headquarters – and get to work. Unlike King Canute he succeeds in accomplishing the impossible, even the miraculous, and Lancashire have had cause to welcome and curse his efforts in turn.

Outwardly, Bert Flack may appear a hard task-master. He certainly has a command over the Queen's English that any sergeant major would approve. He is brusque to both players and members alike. At times he has been known to tell committee officials where they get off. To young spectators he is something of a bogey man. To old ones he is a bugbear. A realist and a perfectionist he may well be. But with all his faults he has few equals and certainly no betters in the arts and crafts of his groundsman's trade. His bark is much worse than his bite and he symbolizes all that is best in his own particular realm. No doubt players, batsmen and bowlers alike, have clashed with him over the state of the wicket or the weather. Without doubt they will continue to do so. But none will attempt to teach Bert Flack new tricks. He knows the score, in every possible way, and with his charming wife maintaining Old Trafford's reputation for spit and polish off the field Lancashire have no cause for complaint. As a southerner who came north to do a job against the odds he has succeeded magnificently. Outwardly he may not appeal to all. Inwardly he has a heart of gold and a dedication to his job that makes him an outstanding master of his craft. Lancashire are fortunate to have in him a worthy successor to so many good groundsmen who have gone before.

There is another man who cannot be overlooked in any complete survey of Lancashire cricket. Gordon MacLaren Taylor is his name, and his job, officially for the last twenty-five years or more, has been that of official scorer. But Taylor, 'Mac' to all and sundry not only at Old Trafford but wherever Lancashire play, has not only recorded runs, for and against, the wickets of his own and opposing batsmen, and the catches that have been taken, but has also been a 'father' to a countless number of players ever since he arrived at the ground way back in the early 1920s as a youngster prepared to do any odd job. Yet it is no small task Taylor has accomplished. Throughout the years he has listened to the troubles and the problems of batsmen and bowlers alike. Old players have gone to him in search of understanding and often of much needed cash. Youngsters have sought him out for advice on matters ranging from cricket to life itself. None have gone away empty-handed. As a scorer 'Mac' Taylor has been the tops. No man in the game keeps his book cleaner or more legible. And certainly no other scorer can provide the answers to the many requests he gets, especially from the press box, with a more cheerful air or split-second accuracy.

Away from Old Trafford 'Mac' looks after hotel arrangements and pays the bills. He arranges trains and books seats. Nowadays he is a reluctant but ever faithful car traveller – still the man to whom all turn when things are not going as smoothly as they should. It is Taylor's own secret how many disgruntled players he has persuaded to stay with Lancashire or encouraged to leave. He alone knows of the strengths and the weaknesses of many of the big name players who have adorned the county's cricket with distinction. If a man is short of cash he usually turns to Taylor for it. If he is carrying too much around, 'Mac' will relieve him of the responsibility of looking after it. In form and out of it there is not one Lancashire cricketer this last forty years who does not frankly admit an indebtedness to 'Mac'.

In his spare time and especially in the winter months, 'Mac' devotes his attention to the raising of funds by the Auxiliary Association, and no man has given more of his life to Lancashire cricket. And never once has he sought the limelight. When, in 1965, he was granted a testimonial he was so shy and retiring that he would not allow the players to turn out in Sunday matches or risk injury at night time to play in a planned series of benefit games. Without question every Lancashire player and most of the visiting ones would cheerfully have given their time and services for the benefit of 'Mac'. He would not allow it, and in consequence his reward came to little more than £1,300, when it could, and should, have been far bigger. But that is the man.

Essentially one of those behind the scenes, 'Mac' remains a key figure in Lancashire cricket. When disputes have arisen, in the dressing room or in an hotel, the captain has never been loath to call in his scorer to sort out the salient facts and advise accordingly. Over a drink at night or on his occasional visit for a flutter on the dogs Taylor remains the man to turn to in any emergency. Seldom does he get flurried; never does he threaten. He is a man of remarkable patience and even more remarkable achievements. Yet nowhere at Old Trafford or elsewhere will you see tributes to his persuasiveness or his dedication. 'Mac' Taylor has seldom misplaced a run or overlooked a ball in jotting down the vital statistics that mean so much in the game of cricket. Yet it is not what is written or recorded that makes this man so indispensable to the club. It is his willingness to serve and his dedication to duty that have made him what he is – the man with a host of

Lancashire's most recent success, their 1971 victory in the Gillette Cup over Kent. A jubilant skipper, Bond and wicketkeeper Farokh Engineer hold the cup aloft. *Left to right*, P. Lever, B. Wood, F. M. Engineer, J. D. Bond, J. Sullivan, D. Lloyd and J. Simmons

After their victory, a celebration in the dressing room. Jack Bond is 'launched' with champagne; the pourer is Farokh Engineer

Lancashire's staff in 1971. *Standing, left to right*, Wood, Tattersall, Shuttleworth, Kennedy, Sullivan, Snellgrove, Hayes, Lloyd (C. H.), Parker, Simmons, Goodwin, Oldfield (coach). *Seated*, Lloyd (D.), Engineer, Lever, Bond, Pilling, Savahe (assistant coach), Hughes

Above, T. A. Higson in 1934, a power behind the throne for more than thirty years

Above, Major Rupert Howard, Lancashire secretary from 1932 to 1948

Cedric S. Rhoades, present chairman of Lancashire, who has worked wonders in reviving interest in the club

Bert Flack; a revealing study of a master groundsman

secrets. He, and he alone, can justly claim to have seen it all. Yet he never will. He is the 'Mr Faithful' of Lancashire cricket, and when the time comes for him to step aside he will go without fuss, without rancour and certainly without thought of reward. His satisfaction will come from the friendship, the confidence and the goodwill that each and every Lancashire cricketer this last forty years has bestowed upon him. No club ever had a better twelfth man!

23. NAMES MAKE NEWS

Cricket is essentially a team game. Yet nothing illustrates the power of it better than the achievements of those who have played it. Lancashire have a proud record of players who have not only distinguished themselves for their county but also for their country. Batsmen and bowlers alike have achieved cricketing immortality and the names of Lancashire players rank with those of every other cricketing county in the game's Hall of Fame. Ever since the formative years, never a season has gone by without one Lancashire player or another illustrating the fragrance of the Red Rose from a cricketing point of view. Many have carved their names in the record book with mighty batting performances and shattering bowling feats. Some have had one glorious hour of fame and then faded from the scene. Others have climbed to the top and stayed there by the sheer merit of their ability or the force of their personality. Lancashire can be proud of their cricketing heritage. Perhaps they were fortunate in having Neville Cardus to describe their play and players over a decade when cricket flourished and crowds were big. But no writer, even one of Cardus's stature, could create prose that will live for ever without the material upon which it was based. From the giants of old to the stars of today, Lancashire can claim their full share of events on the cricketing field. From Johnny Briggs to Brian Statham they can present a roll of honour second to none.

Briggs represented the all-rounder of great gifts. He was the only Lancashire cricketer to score more than ten thousand runs and take more than two thousand wickets, in a career that began in 1879 and ended in 1900. But Briggs was more than an all-rounder. He was a perfect cricketer and a player of humour as well as skill. A rotund little man often likened to an indiarubber ball, Briggs lured batsmen to destruction by sheer guile. He was a left-hander, and he spun the ball from leg to off against the right-handers, and the other way, of course, to the left-hander. It was said of him that he never made the ball turn viciously. His own answer to that is the complete reply. 'It's not what ah do, it's what t'others think ah do as matters.'

Briggs rolled into action, not raced. His approach to the wicket was short and exceedingly sweet. The purists today might complain his arm was not high enough. His record makes a mockery of that. Guile, in the air and off the pitch, was his trump card. On good wickets and on bad he assessed the demands and met them. Often he was freely punished, but he took it in good part. A laugh at his own expense was one of his greatest assets. It has been said that Briggs was fortunate in that he was at his prime before groundsmen had really learned the art of preparing pitches. It could not have been the reason for his success, for did he not play alongside and in opposition to such great cricketers as W. G. Grace, F. S. Jackson and G. L. Jessop? They were batsmen who can be accounted the best in the land, and Briggs opposed them with success as well as failure. Bowling made small physical demands on the little fellow. Yet that was because he made it so. Had he been so minded and so gifted he would and could have bowled fast. He once said of Walter Brearley, with whom he frequently opened the Lancashire bowling: 'Now that were bowling, fast, straight and terrifying.' There was the highest possible regard from the master slow bowler for the master fast bowler. Briggs looked up at his colleague and marvelled that God could give so much in the way of strength and power to one cricketer and yet deny it to him. But he moulded his career to fit his physical attributes. He was a gay deceiver of a bowler. Brearley typified brute force – yet was never ignorant. Briggs, like Rhodes, his arch rival and counterpart from across the Pennines, took wickets by stealth: courteous yet deadly, greedy yet never hungry. Hour after hour, day after day, year after year, Johnny

Briggs would spin his deceiving web of artful flight and harmful spin. He accepted success with glee and was never loath to celebrate. Yet he knew his moments of despair and reckoned he learnt more from failure than from success.

Briggs had a shrewd brain. From the cricketing point of view it never let him down, though in other walks of life he could neither concentrate nor accommodate. He lived life to the full and died a comparatively young man at the age of forty. For twenty years or so he bowled and batted with tremendous effect for Lancashire and enjoyed every minute he was in the company of cricket or cricketers. Down the years his memory has been treasured by all who saw him and even today there are old-timers on the pavilion side at Old Trafford who can just about recall him in his playing days. But because they were very young at the time they cannot add much to what has been written about a remarkable little cricketer and a highly talented one. He was, perhaps, not the first of his kind and certainly will not be the last, but he is beyond comparison because he was Briggs. Happy-go-lucky no doubt, eccentric in a way, maybe. Casual to the point of waywardness, at times the little man must have sorely tried his captain in the heat of battle. But that he could be relied upon at all times was beyond argument. He proved it so often both as a batsman and a bowler. It was said of him when he died that he had set standards beyond approach, and certainly Lancashire cricket cannot point to any other player with so proud an all-round record and so dynamic an impact upon the game.

Briggs last played for Lancashire in 1900, and it was fifty years later before Old Trafford saw another bowler with the will and the power to oust the name of the little left-hander from the ranks of record-breakers. Brian Statham was the name and he was the complete contrast to Briggs. Lithe, sinewy and destructive, Statham came along to add lustre to both Lancashire and England cricket in an age when it was dominated by professionals. Whereas Briggs shone in the company of numerous high-class and exalted amateurs, Statham succeeded in an era when all cricketers became players and the amateurs ceased to be gentlemen. His was the day of the worker and nobody gave more in the way of determination and effort than Statham, known as George to all and sundry on the big cricket scene. It can be said of Statham, without fear of contradiction, that he bowled best when lacking assistance. Certainly he had no regular partner in the Lancashire attack for the greater part of a career which began in 1950 and ended eighteen years and some 2,060 wickets later.

The Statham saga is one of masterly fast bowling and of much hard work in every cricketing country of the world and under conditions which usually favoured the batsman. What were Statham's virtues? He was no stylist, yet he mastered the best batsmen in the world. He never spared himself from the physical point of view but was always in top gear. His pace, at his best, could be compared to the fastest the game has ever known. He did little with the ball in the modern phraseology of swing or swerve. He was the straightest and perhaps the fastest of them all. And of his many victims none summed it up better than a little Welshman called Willie Jones. The backbone of Glamorgan batting at the time, Jones headed a sensational collapse against Statham; when asked why he and so many of his colleagues had failed he replied with immense feeling. ' 'Twas that man Statham, he bowled too bloody fast!' That was the Statham secret of success. It was not in his nature to bowl wide or slow. Like all truly great players, instinct was his greatest asset. He just knew when, and what, was required. Seldom did he fail to produce it. It cannot be said that he never bowled a long hop or a full toss. But it would require a great deal of research to pinpoint the occasions when Statham erred from the straight and narrow.

Statham was an uncomplicated fellow. Strange as it may seem, he was lazy by nature and liked nothing better than to sit and relax with his feet up and a pint of beer at his elbow when not required for action. On tour he slotted into the scheme of things without demur. His captain's word was his command, and when it came his own turn to be a captain he asked nothing of his men he was not prepared to give himself. A man of quiet humour and whimsical expression, he thought deeply about the game but seldom voiced his thoughts aloud. When asked for an opinion he would give it and act accordingly. There came a time towards the end of his career when Lord's decided to restrict a side's first

innings to eighty-five overs in an effort to produce more aggressive cricket and there grew up a brigade of players who argued
the pro's and con's of the experiment and came to the con-
clusion that it was not really necessary to dismiss a batsman if
he could be contained or restricted from the scoring point of
view. The uncanny situation arose when it was considered not
politic to try and get a man out, just so long as he could be contained. In the Lancashire dressing room one morning the time
came for a discussion of the tactics needed to tide over the last
few overs without conceding the opposition too many runs. Seven
wickets were down and although one batsman of repute remained
the others were not considered of any great moment. Accordingly,
plans were being laid to keep the better batsman quiet and work
on the other. 'What do you think, George? It's you that will
have to bowl at him', was the jackpot question put to Statham.
'What do I think? I reckon I'll just knock his bloody castle
over . . . that'll be the best way of containing him,' answered the
poker-faced fast bowler. And he promptly went out to do it.

The direct approach can be classed as Statham's cricketing
creed, and he lived by it. A dropped catch or a rejected lbw
appeal brought no recriminations and certainly no sort of gesture.
Statham was not that sort of cricketer. He welcomed a tilt at the
best batsmen, and was never happier than when bowling at Colin
Cowdrey or Peter May. On one occasion, when Kent entertained
Lancashire at Gravesend, Statham stayed the night with
Cowdrey, who next morning set about his guest with a tremendous flurry of boundary shots. For once Statham was collared,
and when asked his version of the interlude at lunch time George
replied without a flicker of a smile, 'Oh, he was just making me
pay for bed and breakfast.' A delightful character and a truly
great fast bowler; that was Brian Statham, the man who broke all
Lancashire bowling records when he outshone Johnny Briggs
after he had reigned supreme for fifty years. One was fast, the
other slow. Between them they represented bowling at its very
best.

In between Briggs and Statham came a host of other mighty
cricketers, batsmen and bowlers alike. Placing them in order of
merit or judging them on figures is no real criterion of skill or

class. Each and every one of them played his part in the story of Lancashire cricket. No doubt none did more than the majestic Archie MacLaren. He held sway from 1890 until 1914 and was hailed not only as a master batsman but a born captain. There must have been something that was different about MacLaren. He gave to his county's cricket a lustre that cannot be compared to anything before or since. Cardus said of him that 'he strode the field with dignified majesty', and he must have been a veritable master of the arts in all the cricketing attributes of his own and everybody else's day. His immortal innings of 424 against Somerset at Taunton in 1895 pays tribute to his dedication and throws light upon his ability to play shots. It also serves to stress his fitness and his physique. A great batsman he undoubtedly was – and a captain second to none. For England and for Lancashire he ruled in his own inimitable way. His was the day of several superb amateur cricketers and many masterly professional ones. Yet each and everyone of them accepted MacLaren as his captain and voted him the best of all time. Even the difficult Sydney Barnes confessed to a willingness to work harder for MacLaren than for anybody else. 'He was hard but he was fair,' said Barnes, and that was quite a tribute coming from a hard man himself. Yet there was more to it than that. There must have been, for the simple reason that MacLaren himself was not an easy man to live with. Certainly, Lancashire found him an expensive acquisition even as an amateur, and at one time he was engaged as the club's assistant-secretary purely and simply as a means of qualifying him for extra money. In the days when golden sovereigns were the currency of an easy-going world, it is on record that MacLaren earned more than £40 a week as an amateur in first-class cricket.

A man of military bearing, with a bristling moustache and a stern approach to discipline, MacLaren was able to walk alongside such magnificent cricketing figures as W. G. Grace, Lord Hawke, Lord Harris and Sir Stanley Jessop. He was said to have hit harder than Gilbert Jessop at times and both George Hirst and Wilfred Rhodes confessed to being 'more than a little concerned when Mister MacLaren got set'. Such an admission from two Yorkshiremen without peer in their own cricketing sphere speaks volumes for the power MacLaren enjoyed in his best days. At home or on tour, he demanded and was accorded respect without loss of dignity on anyone's part. Mere figures, some 15,735 runs for Lancashire alone, hide rather than stress the magnificence that was MacLaren. He, above all others, needed no reference to figures to confirm his complete mastery. Few bowlers could really claim to get the better of him consistently and one choice remark he made to Hirst in a Yorkshire-Lancashire match years ago serves to illustrate the point. 'You are bowling well, George, but not well enough,' said the Lancashire captain to a bowler who had just got rid of R. H. Spooner and J. T. Tyldesley at next to no cost! Was this arrogance or bluff? MacLaren's friends insisted he was never arrogant, if at times a little unbearable, and they maintained he did not know the meaning of the word bluff as applied to cricket. Can we be sure? That he never lacked faith in his own ability goes without saying. That he could not tolerate inefficient standards on the part of anybody else appears certain. Yet without question Archie MacLaren must be accounted the ruler of all he surveyed.

But what of Hornby and Barlow, to say nothing of Spooner and of Sharp? They were all great batsmen and all capable of big scores and stylish strokes. Spooner, in particular, was said to be the perfect stroke player, an aristocrat in cricket's Golden Age. Undoubtedly Spooner was a delight to the eye and a magnificent fieldsman, as well as a man of infinite charm. He brought a touch of the country to Lancashire cricket and was more at home at Aigburth than at Old Trafford. He needed trees and lawns to match his splendour, not gaunt walls and mill chimneys. Sharp was more the bull dog than the greyhound. As an international on both the cricket and the soccer fields he had great gifts, as did his Everton colleague, the staid and solid Makepeace. The Hornbys brought a business air to their cricket. They looked what they were, really good players intent upon the job at hand, and few opening pairs could earn immortality in rhyme as Hornby and Barlow did, as 'run stealers flickering to and fro'. The batting Tyldesleys, Johnny and Ernest, were dapper little batsmen, stroke players and yet not without aggressive pugnacity. J. T. was a dignified little man with a whiskery moustache, who brought to professional cricket all that is best from the skill and discipline point of view. A long innings from Johnny Tyldesley was a lesson in deportment, an exhibition without blemish, immensely pleasing to the eye and gratifying to the mind. Ernest came later and signified a changing world. His was the day when the senior professional was the game's shop steward and the captain's right-hand man. Strange bed-fellows in modern parlance, but true of the cricketing days between the two world wars. If an innings by J. T. was a lesson in deportment, one from Ernest hinted at splendour in unsuspected places and of a fighting tenacity of purpose so essential if a batsman was to be accounted of the highest class. Whereas Johnny could be well likened to the leader of the orchestra, Ernest was a very efficient trombonist, putting the accent where it really belonged and enlivening the proceedings when called upon. Between them they gave much to be treasured in Lancashire's cricketing archives.

24. IN GOODLY COMPANY

Lacking inches the Tyldesleys none the less played with the big fellows and were in no way inferior. They treated fast bowlers with due deference but seldom gave way. Their attitude to slow bowlers, and none more so than those from Yorkshire, was one of appreciation. They acknowledged the skills and applauded the arts – yet contrived to master them, and succumbed gracefully when failing to do so. Figures could be quoted to show that Johnny and Ernest Tyldesley were the most productive Lancashire batsmen of all time. Each scored over thirty thousand runs, though neither needed the book to confirm their abilities. They dwelled in goodly company and embellished it. Who could ask for more?

The bowling Tyldesleys, Richard and James, were men of girth and magnificence. They hailed from the prolific Bolton League nursery and were not related to the batting brothers, although they played alongside them and earned distinction their own way. James was less successful than Dick but contributed much under more testing conditions. The spinners of Dick Tyldesley were happily blessed with the support of McDonald's pace and Parkin's guile. It meant much to him. Wilfred Rhodes always insisted that the bulky Richard did not really spin the ball. He maintained, and proved it out in the middle, that if you played forward to him you could master him. If you played back you were prone to error – and to lbw decisions against his quickish top-spinner. For a man of immense bulk – he weighed some sixteen stone – Richard was a very agile close-to-the-wicket fieldsman. He was also a persuasive talker and a great asset to Parkin. Between them they talked batsmen galore to their doom.

McDonald was the fast bowling thoroughbred. The dark and handsome Australian was the personification of all that was best in his field. His action was well-nigh perfect. His run-up was more of a glide than an advance. His wrist was cocked like a cobra's head at the moment of delivery and his pace was a sight for the cricketing gods. In the mood, and he was a man of many moods, McDonald could run through a side, and more than one captain took pains to goad the Australian into action by subtle hints and muttering about his power.

It was not quite the same with Barnes. The great Sydney was not a fast bowler in the true sense of the word. Long before the expression ' seaming ' came into cricket, Barnes was demonstrating the dangers of bowling at a brisk medium pace and mingling it with an ability to cut the ball on pitching. He could move it from leg stump to off, or off stump to leg, and disguise his intentions with outsize hands and tremendously strong wrists. There was nothing classical or poetical about his run-up but it was economical and highly successful. Barnes needed a good captain. He found one in MacLaren and was at his best in the few years he devoted to Lancashire cricket under the great man. Nothing but the best would do for Barnes. Tall, gaunt and tremendously strong in his heyday, he could never take things easy or bowl below his best. No matter what the match, if it was worth playing it was worth winning – and Barnes made sure it usually was won.

Barnes was not popular among his fellow professionals because he was more of an individualist than a team man. League cricket, as a club professional with all its attendant responsibilities, suited Barnes best. He tried hard to settle down to the demanding routine of top-class cricket but was never really happy in it. He was a perfectionist. His field placing was exact and exasperating. His appeals were quiet but all-demanding. His victims were made to feel small, yet Barnes had his moments of humanity. He would encourage a young player with talent but had no time for the slap-happy batsman. He disliked exhibitionism and once took himself off in a charity match when opposing Learie Constantine, then at his zenith in league cricket. A big crowd gathered to watch the duel between Barnes and Constantine, but they were doomed to disappointment after a couple of overs. They never knew the reason but those who played in the match did. It was a golden rule in those sort of matches never to dismiss Constantine cheaply. The West-Indies all-rounder was the man the crowd had come to watch and with nothing at stake most bowlers were happy to oblige. Not Barnes. He asked once for lbw against Constantine and a second time for a catch at the wicket. Refused his appeals, he took his sweater from the umpire and told his captain: 'I, too, have a reputation to consider!' Years later, when in semi-retirement on the north Wales coast, Barnes was asked to play in a charity game but refused. The president of the local club went along to plead with the master bowler as one professional man to another; he was a master-builder, and Barnes listened to what he had to say, agreeing, as one professional man to another, to play if the president would return the favour. 'I will do you a favour and play if you will do me a favour in return and build me a house,' said Barnes. The point was not pursued and the match went on without the master fast bowler.

That was Barnes, and his attitude to cricket and to life. Lancashire's loss was the league's gain but the county had much to thank the neighbouring leagues for. And they owed most to the Bolton League, not the all-powerful Lancashire League or the more popular Central Lancashire League. Charles Hallows was typical of the batsmen the Bolton area sent to county cricket. He followed his uncle to Old Trafford and became the only Lancashire batsman ever to hit a thousand runs in May. Left-handed and stylish in all he did, Hallows was a professional with the flair of an amateur. He had something of Spooner and a touch of MacLaren about him. He seldom appeared to hit the ball hard yet scored runs galore and stroked them beautifully on both sides of the wicket. No bowler could feel hard done by when punished by the easy might of the left-hander. His cover drive was accomplished with an apologetic air and the leg glance with a delicacy savouring on the accidental. Yet Hallows was consistent as well as graceful. He looked the part of an opening batsman. Tall, dark and good looking in a sporting way, he could never play an ugly shot. He was best when in an attacking mood but he could defend, and do it stylishly, on bad wickets. He was a batsman who could never shirk a challenge, and even in the tense atmosphere of a roses clash with Yorkshire between the wars was known to hit a six before lunch. Needless to say he was quickly admonished by his more responsible partner, the dour and dogged Harry Makepeace.

Between them, Hallows and Makepeace made up the perfect opening pair, and few counties escaped lightly against one or the other. Hallows was the cricketing artist, Makepeace the artisan. This shrewd little Yorkshireman, with the broken nose of a boxer, was Lancashire's answer to Emmot Robinson. He knew all the tricks of the trade and avoided most of the risks. He became known as a master stone-waller but could play shots when the occasion demanded them. He was the complete foil to the flamboyant Hallows at the other end. Hallows and Makepeace, along with Ernest Tyldesley and Frank Watson, were the cornerstone on which Lancashire built their hat-trick of championship successes in the 1920s, and with these dependable batsman linked to bowlers of the calibre and power of McDonald, Dick Tyldesley and Parkin, it only remained for the captaincy of Leonard Green to complete a perfect cricketing combination.

There were some who likened this successful Lancashire team to a cricketing machine but that was unfair. No mechanical device could bat like Hallows or bowl like McDonald. Green's major occupation was keeping the peace and this he did admirably, fighting for his men at all times, but demanding and obtaining respect and discipline even if there were times when the side's reputation for enjoying themselves gained more publicity than their playing record. As Dick Tyldesley used to put it: 'It's a great life if you don't weaken, but a man's got to let off steam now and again. There's a time for playing and a time for working and skipper sees we do both.' It made sense and it brought results. The burly Tyldesley also excelled on one occasion, when, after taking a terrific hammering from Don Bradman, he was asked his opinion of the then young and up and coming Australian batsman. Without a flicker of a smile the Lancashire bowler said: 'He's a great player – but he's no bloody good for the likes o' me!' In later years many other bowlers were to agree wholeheartedly with the Lancashire spinner.

George Duckworth played another vital part in the team Green led so well. The little wicket keeper was always a cheerful soul and his skill behind the stumps meant much to bowlers, fast and slow alike. His cockily shouted appeals enlivened many a drab spell, but Duckworth had more to offer than a cheerful countenance and an amazing ability to do his job behind the wicket. He possessed a keen cricketing brain and was often the key man in the tactical talks that used to be a feature of Lancashire's cricket in those exciting days. The little fellow from Warringon missed nothing as he crouched behind the stumps. He could read a bowler's intention as well as the batsman's, and some of his catches against the pace of McDonald bordered on the miraculous. His ability to take the spin of Tyldesley and Parkin was almost as uncanny as his reception of McDonald's thunderbolts. The smallest man on the side was by no means the least significant as Lancashire proudly won their three championships in a row.

In later years Ducky brought his great gifts to bear in an advisory capacity not only to his county but also his country. To see him occupying the scorer's box in Australia was to observe a master tactician thinking things out. At intervals Duckworth would go down to the dressing room with words of wisdom as well as lists of figures. He missed nothing of the action, even if he was remotely placed, and many an England batsman has profited from his canny habit of spotting a bowler's weakness or lack of control.

When Green's team broke up and Peter Eckersley took over,

men like Paynter, Washbrook and Oldfield accepted the run-scoring roles, and Pollard and Phillipson came along to share the bowling chores with Sibbles and Iddon, to say nothing of Hopwood, one of the few Lancashire players to do the hundred wicket and thousand run double. Paynter came on the scene somewhat late. He was past the first flush of youth when he finally fought his way into the side, but he soon made an impact and brought a touch of pugnaciousness to Lancashire's middle-order batting with his orthodox but telling brand of stroke play. Left-handed like Hallows, Paynter had little pretentions to style. But there was never a better fighter or harder worker. For a little fellow he hit hard and could not be bettered in the field. He had to assume a lot of responsibility whilst Washbrook and Oldfield were feeling their way, and he seldom let the side down. It was the same when Paynter played for England. He could be relied upon to get runs when they were needed most, and it is now part of cricketing history how he got out of a hospital bed to save England in a test against Australia at Brisbane. That was Paynter's trademark. He was always busy and always willing and did his native Lancashire village of Oswaldtwistle proud in a career that was at its height when the second world war stopped play for five long years.

In the main, only five Lancashire players bridged the gap between 1939 and the full-scale resumption of play in 1946, when Hitler and his hordes had finally been vanquished. Cyril Washbrook and Winston Place represented experienced batsmanship, and Dick Pollard, Eddie Phillipson and Len Wilkinson were the bowlers who came back to usher in a new cricketing decade. Norman Oldfield, Albert Nutter and Paynter decided against a return, and so did Bill Farrimond, the man who took over from Duckworth behind the wicket and played for England whilst still a Lancashire reserve. There were others who had sampled first-class cricket but had very limited experience. Bill Roberts, John Ikin and Gordon Garlick came into this category, and, all, bar Wilkinson, who simply could not recover his prewar brilliance, played a part in the essential rebuilding.

But one man stands out alone as a batsman in this era. Washbrook must be ranked with the greatest who ever took guard for

149

the county and he was at his best when cricket was making the most of the demands made upon it by a sport-starved public from 1946 to 1950. These were vintage years for 'Washy'. He was first choice for England, and along with Len Hutton made up an opening batting combination feared by all bowlers. Yet Washbrook's best work was undoubtedly for his county rather than for his country. He was that cricketing rarity, a batsman who mingled style with power, and he rode roughshod over the county grounds of this country in the immediate postwar years. A man with a jaunty air, Washbrook was often accused of being arrogant and sometimes humourless. There was something in these allegations, but let no man decry Washbrook. He was, without doubt, one of the finest batsmen ever to wear the Red Rose cap, and he was also one of the most respected.

It was Washbrook who eventually broke with tradition to become Lancashire's first ever professional captain, but it was as a free-scoring and attractive batsman that he made his mark. The record books show he hit over 27,000 runs for his county and hammered out some seventy-six centuries in the course of a memorable first-class career. He excelled at the square drive and the hook, and fielded as well as most in the covers or in the deep. If he was suspect it was against pace, and of all the postwar bowlers it was Lindwall and Miller who caused him most concern. Lindwall always maintained that he could tempt Washbrook to hook and get out, and there was something in this charge, although the fiery Australian bowler knew what it was to suffer at Washbrook's hands. So did most of the other top-class bowlers, and wherever Lancashire went in the immediate postwar years they provided attractive as well as punishing batsmanship.

It was inevitable that Washbrook should outshine any other batsman in the team and it was always Place's lot to walk in the shadow of his England partner. Whereas Washbrook was by his very nature aggressive and domineering as a batsman, Place did his best work by stealth. He was undoubtedly a technically correct batsman. He was brought up in the hot-bed of Lancashire League cricket alongside some prominent professionals and the Rawtenstall man learned his game the hard way. On bad wickets he was far more reliable than his partner. On good ones he

plodded rather than strolled along, but there was much to admire
in the batting of Place. Like Washbrook, he wore his cap at a
jaunty angle and would stand no criticism of Lancashire cricket
or the men who made it. He was a man with a whimsical sense
of humour and started many an off-the-field argument just for the
devil of it. The quiet man of the side, Place was by no means an
insignificant one. He had a cricketing brain and could analyse a
bowler with uncanny exactness. In many ways he was the perfect
foil for Washbrook, and between them they gave a distinguished
air to Lancashire cricket when it needed it most.

The pair of them set the batting standards and left it to
Pollard to look after the bowling. This burly West Houghton
man was typical of the Bolton League where he learned the game,
and it was not for nothing that he earned the cricketing nickname
of 'th'owd chain horse'. It was a tribute both to his stamina and
his will power. Day after day, year after year, Pollard used both
the new ball and the old with deadly effect. He was not a fast
bowler by comparison with McDonald or Statham, but he was a
mighty valuable one for all that. At his best, when there was a
touch of greenness or a little dampness in the pitch, Pollard
bowled heroically for both his county and his country and took
over a thousand wickets. Figures, however bear no relation to the
merit or the determination with which Pollard went to work. Like
most red-haired men he had a touch of temper and his bowling
was all the better for it. A cheery soul, he was never found wanting and it was not until Alec Bedser came along that English
cricket was able to pension Pollard off. Like many more of his
era, Dick Pollard lost the best years of his cricket life to wartime
service, but he was fit to dwell in the highest cricketing company.
No county or country ever had a greater trier, and Pollard's contribution to the scene was a notable one. He was one of the
game's indispensables, a bowler who never knew what it meant
to give up. Hard labour was usually his lot and he shouldered the
burden magnificently, to bridge two sporting decades.

Phillipson, like Pollard, lost his best years in fighting for a
nobler cause, but he was a fast bowler capable of testing any
batsman with a pace and a swing above the average. That he did
not grace the game as long as most was hardly his fault, but when

he faded from the Old Trafford scene at the end of the 1948 season it was primarily because Lancashire placed their faith in spin rather than pace.

25. THREE YOUNG SPINNERS

Lancashire had discovered and encouraged Roy Tattersall, Malcolm Hilton and Bob Berry to try their luck in first-class cricket, and all three played for England almost as soon as they had won county caps. Tattersall, tall, angular, and blessed with big hands and strong legs, made his impact as an off-spinner, and could use the new ball almost as effectively as the old one. Like so many of Lancashire's best players, he was a product of the Bolton League, and in twelve years, from 1948 to 1960, he was a thorn in any batsman's side. His height enabled him to get lift and his action encouraged movement off the seam. Add to this an amazing ability to cut or spin the ball, and Tattersall was a very gifted bowler. Seven times he topped the hundred wicket mark in county cricket, but figures never really revealed the deadliness of his attack. Had he been fortunate enough to play under more sympathetic captains he might well have broken all records. Alas, with the exception of Nigel Howard, who was too young and inexperienced to make the most of his ability, Tattersall had to struggle along under men who could not make up their minds whether he was a spinner or a cutter. Washbrook was one, and Hutton another. They gave Tattersall plenty of work but never really got down to the task of understanding a unique and ever-willing bowler. It was always the opposition who paid this lanky Bolton man the greater tributes and none had higher regard for him than the South African batsmen of his day. To them he was always a man to be feared, but often his own captains and colleagues were blind to his needs and his deeds. It says much for Tattersall's spirit that he seldom complained, but bowled his overs economically and tidily, often with great profit and rarely without some satisfaction. A bowler admired for his style and his willingness to work hard at all times, Roy Tattersall gave far more to cricket than he got out of it. He produced the goods but gained little reward. He moved in the top cricketing circles yet was never really in the swim. Why, was always something of a mystery. Maybe it was because of his own innate shyness and desire to shun the limelight. None the less he was one of the best.

Malcolm Hilton was in personality just the opposite. A left-hander from Werneth in the Central Lancashire sphere, he went to Old Trafford straight from school and started off his first-class career with the biggest possible bang – by dismissing Bradman twice in one match! Rather quicker than most left-handed spinners, Hilton was always dangerous and on helpful pitches often unplayable. He never lacked confidence and frequently paid the penalty for being over-confident. He matched his bowling with superb close-to-the-wicket fielding and with the bat he could hit or defend as the occasion demanded. 'Benny', as Hilton became known, enjoyed his cricket immensely and had the happy knack of conveying that enjoyment to the spectators. He was never consistent enough to be ranked with Briggs or even with Roberts, but he did much good work for Lancashire.

And so did Berry. This little fellow from the Lancashire and Cheshire League was the orthodox left-hand spinner. He harnessed length to flight and spin, and always presented problems if the pitch was at all helpful. He had his greatest moments against the West Indies and the Indians, but tired of fighting for a regular place alongside Hilton and Tattersall. He migrated first to Worcestershire and then to Derbyshire, and was always a much better bowler than his figures suggested. What is more, he was an ideal team man, and a character with a sense of infectious humour that did much to lighten the dark days through which every cricket side must travel.

Since he departed, and once Hilton and Tattersall had followed him, Lancashire cricket has lacked good spinners. The leagues cannot now provide them, and are, in point of fact, not producing either batsmen or bowlers in the quantities and qualities of old. If Hilton, Tattersall and Berry represented the best in the spinning line, Lever, Shuttleworth and Higgs provided the pace. All three became England, as well as Lancashire bowlers, and it was Higgs who gave Statham the only strong support he ever had. A Staffordshire League product, Higgs was from the Pollard mould. He was strong and he was willing. It was his lot to lend aid rather than provide shocks, but he had his moments and did much to help get Lancashire cricket back on the right lines after years in the sidings. Lever and Shuttleworth are still making their way. Each has strength to foster ambition and neither will lack opportunity. Their best days have yet to come.

Turning to the batsmen, none did better than Geoff Pullar. Like Hilton, he came from the Werneth club to Old Trafford and soon made his mark as a stylish left-hander with a touch of Hallows and trace of Paynter in his make-up. Blessed with a placid temperament and infinite patience, Pullar became the solid rather than spectacular left-hander of old. He was essentially an opening batsman, who liked to take his time and dabble with the theory of the game. Yet he is the only Lancashire batsman to hit a test century for England at Old Trafford. This solidly built Oldhamer achieved something that eluded the best batsmen the county ever produced. He succeeded where MacLaren, the Tyldesleys, Hallows, Paynter and the rest failed – and yet he was never really in their class.

Marner was another Lancashire recruit from the Oldham area – and one who was never allowed to play the game his own way. A big fellow, and a natural striker of the ball, Marner had great gifts. He could bowl as well as bat and was equal to the best from the slip fielding point of view. Yet he never really made the grade. He suffered from the lack of inspired leadership and shrewdly administered discipline. He once hit a half-century of great potential against Kent at Gravesend and punished severely the leg-spinners of Doug Wright. When asked if he had spotted the England spinner's googly he answered, with youthful in- nocence, 'Ah didn't know he bowled one.' Advised to pay a little more attention to theory than practice, Marner was never quite the same player, and, lacking the right sort of encouragement, he faded from the scene.

He was not alone in this. Bob Barber, David Green and Duncan Worsley were three young university blues who all had much to offer and did their best to establish themselves. Barber

154

failed dismally with Lancashire but eventually found form and favour with Warwickshire and England. A talented all-rounder, he was handicapped by too much responsibility too early and a lack of understanding at Old Trafford. The same can be said of Worsley and of Green. They had the ability but received precious little encouragement to employ it. Captains like MacLaren, Green and Bond would, without a doubt, have steered these promising young hopefuls to the top.

The mention of Bond in the same category as MacLaren and Green might raise eyebrows in many cricketing quarters, but the present Lancashire captain has clearly established his right to be considered one of the best. A batsman who had to struggle desperately to earn his place in the side, Bond was as surprised as most others when appointed in 1968, but he proved himself the man for the job within a matter of weeks. Perhaps it is because he had known adversity himself that he has been able to steer others through the doldrums into the light. Different from Green inasmuch as he had no previous example of leadership or man management, Bond has won through on the strength of his own tremendous regard for fair play and team spirit. He accepted the captaincy knowing full well the snags that lay ahead. He had to build a new team. Youthful newcomers had to be discovered and encouraged. Experienced overseas signings had to be introduced and yet not embarrassed. Lancashire had gained a reputation for enduring rather than enjoying their cricket and none knew better than Bond the consequences of failure. He was fortunate in being appointed by the right man. He accepted responsibility as well as leadership. Backed by a chairman and committee geared to a progressive if somewhat permissive age, Bond was told to do things his way. That his way was the right one has been proved by the winning of two John Player League championships and two Gillette Cup successes in successive years. Twice Lancashire have finished third in the county championship under Bond, and the time may soon come when they win what he describes as 'the big one' as well.

But there is more to good cricket than the winning of cups, and Bond is never tired of instructing his men to go out and enjoy themselves. He places great faith in enjoyment! It breeds happiness and contentment and with the skipper setting the right example Lancashire cricket is now happy cricket. Individuals are important but team work is top priority. Discipline comes naturally and differences of opinion are settled the democratic way. No player need be afraid of saying his piece and none is denied the right to put forward suggestions. Harsh words there may well be on occasions but all are said behind closed doors. Good cricket has brought its own reward. Better terms and more security have been sought and obtained on Bond's appeal. Big crowds have also brought satisfaction, and where once there was apathy and distrust there is now enthusiasm and cooperation. Players and committee members pull together in the common cause and whilst Bond and his men have been busy on the field, Chairman Rhoades and his committee have been working tremendously hard not only to find the ways and means of financing the new deal but also of enlarging its scope. Through the newly-formed Lancashire Cricket Association all the cricketing bodies of the county are being drawn closer and closer together and Old Trafford is now the meeting place of all who work for cricket in Lancashire.

Inevitably, old traditions have been breached and old customs sacrificed. It may well be true that the pavilion side is no longer the holy of holies – the place where standards of dress were once measured by tall hats, frock coats, and then collars and old-school ties. Now a member is at liberty to make himself comfortable. An open-neck shirt is an indication of freedom of movement as well as freedom of action. A man may now quench his thirst and still watch the cricket, and before very long a man and his wife may soon be sitting side by side on seats that have been exclusively male preserves for a century or more. Does this really matter? Is it a cause for regret that Clive Lloyd was born in Guyana and not Garstang: that Farokh Engineer hails from Bombay and not Blackpool? The minority may express doubts but the majority have overruled them. It is the democratic way of things and Old Trafford is today the meeting place for all who like good cricket – the venue where creed and race are subordinate to good sportsmanship.

26. THE FOREIGN LEGION

Lancashire have never been averse to recruiting outside aid. When the native born cricketer has not been available they have gone out and secured the outsiders. Many of them, in the early days, came from neighbouring counties and a good number of Yorkshiremen have made the trip across the Pennines to add lustre to Lancashire cricket. Recruits from abroad are now the aim of most counties who have gaps to fill and cannot find the men among their own clubs and leagues. Lancashire, be it noted, wholeheartedly agreed to lead the new demand when, in readiness for the 1968 season, they persuaded the other counties to widen the qualification laws and allow overseas players into English cricket on special registrations. They imposed a limit and, in their own case, stressed it was merely for stop-gap purposes – to strengthen weak spots until a local-born youngster could be found to do the job. Lancashire's persuasive advocacy of this new look brought the world's best players into the county cricket orbit, and although there was some unseemly bargaining for the services of Gary Sobers as the first and most sought-after 'importation', the scheme has worked well and English cricket has prospered.

The big thing, of course, is to see there is no large takeover. County cricket in this country must essentially be English cricket and Lancashire are well aware of the fact. They have, in Farokh Engineer and Clive Lloyd, two of the most attractive players in the world and they have blended them into their team without loss of faith, dignity or support. Whether there will be other overseas signings remains to be seen. The club's aim is for Lancashire to be self-supporting, but should the occasion and the necessity arise no doubt steps will be taken to plug the gap once more. It was not always so. For many years the county could have had their pick of the international cricket market almost without cost, for in the Lancashire and Central Leagues were the best players from the best cricketing countries. All that was needed was a qualification period and this, of course, was in process whilst the stars were fulfilling their contracts with the league clubs.

Lancashire closed their eyes to the availability of these men but other counties came along and secured their services, often at bargain prices, and without the cost of their air or sea passages to this country.

At the time, Lancashire cricket was struggling along in an attempt to be self-supporting and the only really notable overseas recruit from 1947 to 1967 was the Australian all-rounder, Ken Grieves. He came to play Lancashire League cricket with Rawtenstall as a substitute for Keith Miller in 1946, and stayed on to make his mark both in cricket and in the football world. As a Lancashire cricketer and a goalkeeper with Bury, Bolton and Stockport County, Grieves graced the northern sporting scene for a decade and is still doing a great job of work in the Central Lancashire League as a club captain and encourager of young-sters. An entertaining batsman and a top-class fieldsman, Grieves could also bowl leg-spinners with effect in his early days, and, of course, in the crisis of the mid-1960s, the Australian captained the county for two years. His best work was undoubtedly done in his early years at Old Trafford, and with Edrich and Ikin he made up a trio of close-to-the-wicket fieldsmen few counties have been able to better, before or since.

Grieves, of course, was not the first Australian to qualify for Lancashire via the leagues of the county. McDonald beat him to it after the triumphant Australian tour of 1921 when he and J. M. Gregory blasted out the England batsmen in test afer test. Nelson, always the trend-setters in tempting the top-class cricketers into the leagues, signed McDonald and played him for two years until he was qualified by residence to play for Lancashire. Few, spectators or officials, saw anything wrong with this method of strengthening the Lancashire team and two more colonials, as they were in those days, made occasional appearances with the county. Horrocks, from Australia, was one, and Hall, from South Africa, was another.

Neither Horrocks nor Hall made any great impact, for they were trying their luck when Lancashire cricket was at its strongest, and it is in more recent years that the real opportunities have arisen. None have slipped more gracefully into the scene than Engineer and Lloyd. The Indian wicket keeper took no real persuading to switch from his native Bombay to Old Trafford. He liked Lancashire's home from the moment he first set eyes on it as a member of the Nawab of Pataudi's touring team in 1967; and it did not take him long to make up his mind that he could have a better cricketing future in this country than in India. He is, without doubt, the best of his kind in the world today, and if he has not yet hit his best form with the bat he remains one of the most attractive stroke players in the game. His wicket keeping is on a different plane to any Lancashire have had before. Duckworth was sound, highly skilled and often spectacular. Farrimond was the efficient and always reliable wicket keeper who could get runs in his own dour way. Both contributed much to Lancashire cricket, yet they could not make it sparkle to the extent Engineer has done. The Indian freely admits to being a showman. He likes to do everything the spectacular way, yet he contrives to make it look not only safe but frequently easy. His uncanny anticipation and reading of a batsman's mind and a bowler's intention enables him to be in the right place at the right time, and many a top-class batsman has left the crease completely bewildered at being caught behind the wicket off what he considered a well-played and ideally placed leg glance. There are times, in fact, when Engineer touches the heights of genius – and occasions, especially with the bat, when he infuriates by a lack of patience and understanding of the needs of the moment. Yet it cannot be denied or even doubted he is very much an entertainer as well as a cricketer. He has brought a touch of Indian magic to the Lancashire scene and slotted into the scheme of things so well that he has broken down all barriers and become one of the boys in every possible way.

The same can be said of Clive Lloyd. The West Indies left-hander is more than a cricketer, he is the personification of all that is best in sport. As an individualist he has no peer among batsmen or fieldsmen. As a team man he is ever-willing, and often anxious to escape the spotlight. His build, that of a man with immense physical attributes, does not prevent him moving at terrific speed. The fact that he wears glasses, or sometimes plays in contact lenses, does not prevent him seeing the ball and dealing with it in the manner of a true genius. His creed is simple. 'If I can see the ball I can hit it or catch it', is the basic principle behind his game. Blessed with a placid temperament and a nonchalent regard for the opposition, Lloyd is the complete cricketer. He bats with delightful ease yet generates terrific power. And his fielding at cover point is of cat-like grace and bulldog power. The man who hesitates over a run with Lloyd around is committing cricket suicide. His throwing ability is phenomenal. Not only does he aim with tremendous might but also with crashing accuracy. If he can see the stumps he can hit them. Seldom has so much cricketing talent been endowed in one muscular frame. Yet off the field big Clive is a delightful companion. Not for him the bright lights and the late nights. He seeks his entertainment the simple way. He likes music and is a keen television and film watcher. He drives a car with all the assurance and some of the skill of the racing motorist. And he has a sense of humour that can turn dejection into ecstacy in a split second.

The stories he tells are simple and honest, and he is never averse to listening to or relating stories about the colour of his skin. In the middle he is responsible for many a quiet chuckle and often a loud laugh. One England batsman knows full well the ability of Lloyd to come up with the master retort. Towards the close of one over-limited innings this hard-hitting batsman, then on his way towards a century, enquired of Clive, who was bowling at the time, 'How many more overs to go?' 'Just three, son, take it easy', was the reply. For some reason or other the batsman sought confirmation from the umpire, who readily confirmed the accuracy of the information. 'Satisfied now, son, you've got it in black and white!', came the ready quip from Lloyd, and with it a peal of laughter from those nearest the scene of the action.

Another Lloyd story illustrates his happy-go-lucky attitude to cricket and those who watch it. On his way to Lord's for the Gillette Cup final against Kent the lanky Lancashire player was stopped by a youngster as he approached the Grace Gates. 'Excuse me, Mister Lloyd, have you got a ticket to spare? I'll pay ten pounds for a ten shilling seat before I'll miss this match,' was the plea. Lloyd looked at the youngster, patted him on the head and replied 'Son, for that sort of money you can play in the ruddy match.' And he steered the boy through the gates before the eyes of a gatekeeper who had not the heart to challenge him.

That is Lloyd, the complete cricketer. A century before lunch would please big Clive immensely. A duck first ball would not distress him. Success and failure come alike to this genial West Indies giant who has ambitions to captain his country. He could well achieve it – and the day might also dawn when he captains his adopted county. In the event there will be no outcry, no criticism, and certainly no forebodings, for Clive Lloyd is the perfect gentleman as well as the ideal cricketer. Lancashire chose well when they persuaded him to forsake Haslingden and the Lancashire League for Old Trafford and county cricket. Fears that he might dominate and degenerate the scene were soon dispelled. He had no takeover plans. His aim was simply to merge and become one of the boys. He has succeeded, on the field and off, and Lancashire cricket is all the richer for his presence.

Tribute must also be paid to the many Yorkshiremen who have played their part on the Lancashire cricketing scene. Albert Ward was probably one of the first. He was followed by a steady stream of players, some highly successful, others not too dominating. Harry Makepeace typified the dourness of the Yorkshireman in exile. He lived and played in a time when the game was blessed with many 'characters'. Many of them were created by Neville Cardus and occasionally some other cricketing scribe, but character was not illustrated without the basic ingredient of ability, and Makepeace was tailor-made for the prose of Cardus. His mannerisms and his tactical approach hinted at suspicion – suspicion not only of the opposition but also of the elements and even the frailties of his colleagues. If Makepeace was at his best in the ancient and honourable cricketing battles between Lancashire and Yorkshire, it was, no doubt, because he had a foot in both camps and a fanatical determination to do justice not only to himself but also to the cause.

In Barry Wood, Lancashire today possess just such another cricketing exile. Wood came over the Pennines with the blessing of an old Yorkshire captain and chairman, Brian Sellers, whose professed attitude to Lancashire and its cricketers is to 'give 'em

nowt'. Yet Sellers begged Old Trafford to give Wood a trial. He
badly wanted to see the Ossett man wearing the White Rose cap
but there was no opening at the time, and Sellers knew it. 'Off
you go, lad. Try your luck with Lancashire, but tek it easy when
and if you play against Yorkshire,' were his parting words to a
determined young all-rounder.

Wood made the trip and soon proved his worth. Now he is
one of the most valued members of the side Bond leads. It goes
without saying he retains his native intuition and most of its
dialect. A sentence from Wood is a breath of Yorkshire air, as
bracing as Ilkley Moor and as broad as a Cleckheaton wool-
winder in a November fog. Barry Wood is Harry Makepeace re-
incarnated, and his contributions to Lancashire cricket already
include two centuries in one summer – against Yorkshire. There
are more to come. It cannot be otherwise when a man of Wood's
ability and determination is around. In the hurly-burly of Sunday
League cricket Wood is often relegated in the batting order or
even left in the dressing room. It is an offence against his cricketing pride but it serves to send him out on a Monday morning
vowing vengeance on all and sundry. The time will come when
Lancashire cannot afford to leave Wood out of the reckoning any
day, any week, any year. In addition to his disciplined batsmanship – and he is not the slow-coach a lot of people believe him
to be – the Yorkshireman can bowl at a brisk medium pace with
enough swing and variations in pace and length to dismiss the
best batsmen. He is seldom faulted in the field and never hesitates
to relieve his feelings with a frenzied appeal or a joyful jump.
Garnished by a touch of Indian magic from Engineer, spiced by
the West Indian spirit of Lloyd, and now seasoned by the Yorkshire relish of Wood, Lancashire cricket has more than a mere
international flavour. It has the 'palate' of the gourmet and the
appetite of a hungry wolf. Runs and wickets alone will not satisfy
it. There must also be success in every cricketing sphere. The
meal is only just beginning!

27. THE BEST TEAM

As an exercise for the times when rain stops play or prevents it being started there can be no more fascinating pastime than choosing the best team Lancashire can field and pitting it against the best of any other county. In the nostalgic belief that the generation gap can be bridged and every man chosen at the height of his career one can name a team to delight the eye and the ear of any cricketing spectator. Blend is the vital factor and skill the basic ingredient; style has its place and performance its essential part to play, and there will be no general agreement with any team chosen.

First and foremost must come the naming of the captain – and perhaps this is the easiest task of all. For who could oppose MacLaren? Did he not prove to be the greatest of them all at both county and country level. Few will argue against his ability to lead men or to score runs. None will quibble at his attitude to the job on hand. As a batsman and a tactician he cannot be faulted. As a captain he cannot be opposed. His sense of discipline and determination of purpose may well be foreign to the young cricketers of today. But that they were good for the game and for the club cannot and will not be denied.

Yes, MacLaren is the captain and Washbrook must open the innings with him. Many will prefer Spooner. Some would vote for Hallows. One or two might want to include Hornby and perhaps Barlow, but surely Washbrook is worthy of inclusion among the best who have played for Lancashire. As batsmen of great gifts Washbrook and MacLaren would have much in common. Certainly they would approach the job with the same degree of dedication and responsibility. Each, in his own way and time, dominated the scene and the sight of them together at the start of the Lancashire innings would surely inspire Cardus to come back and write about the game.

If a good start is essential, and it usually is, there is still a great deal to be said for the right supporting cast, and at first wicket down can any selector do better than nominate J. T. Tyldesley? The little man from Worsley is generally regarded as the best of the county's professional batsmen and he would fit in perfectly behind MacLaren and Washbrook. To follow him must come Clive Lloyd, for few can doubt the West Indian left-hander's right to be invited to dwell in the highest company. And think of the great gifts this mighty man would bring to bear as a fieldsman at cover point. Even Washbrook would have to move over to accommodate him.

In the belief that a big total would be necessary to win this cricketing encounter extraordinary, the middle order batting must be given serious thought, and at number 5 there must be competition among many. The vote could go to E. Tyldesley, with Paynter challenging hard, and Sharp not to be ignored. Two Tyldesleys in one side may be something of a luxury but how delightful to be presented with such an embarrassment of riches. A true professional, Ernest, like Johnny, would be an insurance against accidents or a sticky wicket.

To follow must come a man capable of filling two key positions. Engineer, batting sixth and keeping wicket, meets the situation perfectly. His great gifts and spectacular manner would assure him of a tremendous welcome from the crowd that would gather for this impossible but all-enchanting cricketing duel. (And which county, other than Yorkshire, could really provide the ideal opposition?) But back to business. The batting is in good hands and the wicket keeping role assigned, to the general regret of those who saw Duckworth and Farrimond at their best and also recall the valuable contribution Pilling made to the Lancashire scene in its very early days.

Now to the bowling! Pace and spin are available and who could oppose the pairing of McDonald and Statham with the new ball? None other than Barnes, no doubt, but the great S. F. finds a place in the side – as the stock bowler as opposed to the shock bowlers. How fortunate a captain to have Barnes available after an opening spell from McDonald and Statham. The Australian would produce the style and Statham the power. Between them they could and should be a match for the best batsmen in the world, at any given date or time. Statham, with his straightness, and McDonald with his movement, would satisfy all but the most pernicious of critics. Once they had accomplished their task, and surely wickets would have fallen, Barnes could take over and keep one end tight for the rest of the innings. To ask Barnes to bowl tight would not be necessary. He never bowled any other way. A batsman who waited for the long hop or the full toss, even for the half volley off the wicket, would wait in vain. Barnes, under the command of MacLaren, would see to that.

Every good side must have its spinners, preferably one left-hander and one leg-breaker or offbreaker. Briggs would walk into the side as the left-hander. Lancashire cricket is not exactly re-nowned for its quality of spin but Briggs had few superiors on good wickets or bad. His flight was tantalizing, his length variable. His spin was vicious under favourable conditions and testing in others. An ability to bowl for hours on end and also get runs late down in the batting order makes Briggs as automatic a choice as was MacLaren for the captaincy. They played together and often disagreed on both tactics and principles. Yet they respected each other and gave of their best without demur. In between the wars, Hopwood provided the same sort of service as did Briggs, Heap and Dean years before, but there can be no questioning the right of the older man to play in this team of all the talents.

One place remains to be filled. An off-spinner or a leg-spinner? Which is it to be? Dick Tyldesley vies with Ramadhin in one role and Parkin battles with Tattersall in the other. The leg-spinner demands a hard and fast pitch. Old Trafford has pro-vided many of them in the past and could do so again, but on the whole there are more pitches to suit the off-spinner than the leg-spinner whenever Lancashire do battle at their own headquarters. For that reason alone, the last spot must go to the off-spinner, and surely Parkin must get the edge. More than a spinner, yet never a seamer, the Durham-born bowler was capable of bowling six different kinds of deliveries in an over. Tattersall was not quite so versatile though he never failed to present problems. Good batsmen could 'collar' both, but the times when they did so were few and far between. This is the most difficult choice of all and because Parkin was a better batsman and moved more freely in the field he must win the vote over Tattersall. There could never be much in it, but the versatility of one counts for more than the accuracy of the other.

And so the team (in batting order) will be:

A. C. MacLaren
C. Washbrook
J. T. Tyldesley
C. H. Lloyd
E. Tyldesley
F. M. Engineer
J. Briggs
C. H. Parkin
S. F. Barnes
E. A. McDonald
J. B. Statham

A twelfth man must be added and here the field of choice is wide. Paynter would fill the role perfectly and can be accounted unlucky not to win a place in the side. His rivals for the consolation spot could be one of many, and thoughts of such magnificent players as Spooner, Hallows, Watson, Makepeace, Iddon, Place, Duckworth, Farrimond, or the Hornbys, figuring among the reserves must give rise to much speculation, to say nothing of feverish argument. Without a doubt, Lancashire, fielding a team of players steeped in test match traditions as well as proved in the heat of battle, would be a match for any other county also given the licence to choose the best at their best. Yorkshire, no doubt, could field an equally powerful, if not better, combination. Maybe Surrey could and perhaps Middlesex, and Kent too, but Lancashire would go into battle with strong support and undeniable faith in themselves.

28. BATTLES OF THE ROSES

No story of Lancashire cricket would be complete without special reference to the county's matches with Yorkshire. For the simple reason that these annual cricketing battles of the rival roses are special, they must be allocated their own place, and in the belief that the best usually comes last, a full discussion has been pur- posely delayed.

There is nothing better in cricket than a Lancashire and York- shire match. Test matches between England and Australia are, for countless thousands of cricketing enthusiasts, the really big occasions in the game. But in the north of England the atmos- phere on the field and round the ring when Lancashire batsman opposes Yorkshire bowler, and vice versa, underlines the import- ance of the occasion. Ask the players on either side what they think about it and often the reply would be to the effect there are three great moments in the life of every first-class cricketer – the day he makes his début, the first time he plays for England, and his baptism of fire in a Lancashire-Yorkshire match. Which comes first is surely a matter of individual choice, but many will insist that roses cricket brings with it something no other match can provide. People outside the two counties will scoff at this assertion, but in the words of such as Emmott Robinson, Harry Makepeace, Roy Kilner and Winston Place: 'It's nowt to do wi them.' And, of course, it hasn't.

Strictly speaking, when Lancashire meet Yorkshire on the cricket field a game becomes a war, but it was never true, as the hoary old chestnut insists, that the players say good morning on the first day and never speak again except to say 'Ow's Zat?' There is ample evidence to support the belief that conversation pieces are part and parcel of the struggle and even part of the strategy of the duels. Certainly Emmott Robinson, for one, was never backward in expressing his opinion on the strength or the weakness of those who opposed him. Likewise, Dick Tyldesley did not hesitate to urge Yorkshire batsmen to play back instead of forward in the hope of trapping them lbw to his fiery top- spinner.

No 'chatting up the opposition' is accepted as essential propa- ganda for battle purposes. Opinions differ as to when these annual cricketing dog fights really began but that is not of any real importance. That they did and still do represent the high- light of each and every season goes without saying. Perhaps some of the fire and a lot of the character is missing today, but maybe this can be attributed more to the critics than the players. Character, as Cardus was prone to proclaim, persists wherever the game is played – and a roses encounter cannot fail to make this apparent. On the whole, and even the most partisan of Lancashire supporters will be forced to agree, Yorkshire have had the better of these struggles in the past, but Lancashire will never give up hope that soon the trend will be reversed. To do otherwise would be denying cricket its very existence.

Although nowadays the battles are confined to Old Trafford, Leeds and Sheffield, and soon Bramall Lane will be no more as a cricketing venue, the teams have met in some unlikely places, and produced some very unlikely results. Whalley, in Lancashire, for instance, and Holbeck in Yorkshire, too. But it was never the venue that made the match. It was the players and the crowd. Yes, the spectators are more than mere observers when Lancashire do cricketing battle with Yorkshire. Partisanship is accepted, even encouraged, and there was never any lack of tactical knowledge or entertaining wit either on the popular side or in the members enclosure. Whether it is true or not, nothing better illustrates this point than the oft-told story of the two Lancashire die-hards who never missed the chance to watch these seasonal battles. On one occasion Jim and Joe were parted. Jim had business to attend to at home before he could get down to his favourite seat behind the bowler's arm, but Joe kept his place for him. Out of breath, and obviously excited, Jim bustled in just before lunch with a blurted apology on his lips and a sad message to convey. 'Ah geet bad news for thi, lad. Tha wife's gone out with another fellow.' 'Is that so,' said Joe. 'Ah geet bad news for thi, too. Washy's out.' And thus relieved of all tension they settled down to pay their respects to the game in progress!

Personal achievements rank as highly as the match returns in the annals of Lancashire-Yorkshire cricket and each county in turn has cheered the good tidings and suffered the bad. For Lancashire there can be nothing more satisfying than re-telling of the story of that magnificent victory at Leeds in 1924. It goes without saying that Lancashire had batted slowly on the first day. No batsmen ever did otherwise on these occasions. A first innings total of 113 spread over almost four hours cricket against the naggingly accurate bowling of Macauley, Kilner and Rhodes, was in itself a hint at the shape of things to come. At least it was a clear indication this was to be a bowler's match. Yorkshire, equally puzzled by the steadiness of Parkin and Dick Tyldesley, also took their time in winning a lead of seventeen runs before the real fun began on the second afternoon. Again, the three Yorkshire spinners held the upper hand. Making the best possible use of a helpful pitch, they tumbled Lancashire out for seventy-four, but did not hurry in so doing. 'We stood back to admire our handiwork at times,' said Macauley at close of play. And with Yorkshire needing only fifty-seven runs for victory, who could blame him or any other White Rose supporter from gloating over what appeared to be the eventual overthrow of the old enemy. The Lancashire dressing room was the only place where hope survived – and this was based more on a weather forecast than any cricketing prediction. In the press box there was the usual alacrity to write the match off and at least one leading journalist was thinking more in terms of early trains home rather than any cricketing shocks to come when play reopened on the last morning.

All the talk of rain had come to nothing. Lancashire were up against it, but they went out determined to make the going as difficult as possible. They did more. In a matter of a hundred minutes or so Yorkshire were skittled out for thirty-three and Lancashire gained a sensational victory by twenty-three runs. Dick Tyldesley, with a magnificent return of 6-18 was the main destroyer, but Parkin had lent him the accurate assistance demanded and not one Yorkshire batsman had been able to deny Lancashire their day of days. When the score books were audited it was learned that Parkin had match figures of 8-61 and Tyldesley 10-87. The only consolation for Yorkshire was that very few people had turned up to see them humiliated. Thousands had taken it for granted that Yorkshire would win in their own good time and the result was received with very mixed feelings. 'Impossible', insisted some. 'Are you sure?' said others. But there it was, in black and white. Lancashire had gained what was probably their most famous victory ever over the ancient enemy. That total of thirty-three is still Yorkshire's lowest against Red Rose opposition, but looking on the other side of the ledger Lancashire were dismissed for their lowest total at Holbeck way back in 1863. On that black day they mustered a mere thirty.

One G. F. Kemp, later Lord Rochdale, was the first Lancashire batsman to hit a century against Yorkshire as long ago as 1885, and the only double century to the credit of a Lancashire player in these vital cricketing duels is an unbeaten two hundred not out by the stylish Spooner in 1910. Occasionally a Lancashire batsman has been bold enough to hit a century, even two centuries, in a summer against the Yorkshire attack. Washbrook did it in 1948 and so did Bond in 1962, whilst Wood created a bit of cricketing history as recently as 1970 by being the first Yorkshireman to perform such a feat against his native county in roses duels. Pullar, however, has an even better record against the old enemy. In the 1959 season the left-hander hit a roses century at home and away, and then went on to do the same when Yorkshire, as county champions, challenged the Rest at the Oval, to wind up a memorable season. What is more, the following season Pullar hit another roses century just to show Yorkshire that there was at least one Lancashire batsman who relished their attack.

There have been many remarkable bowling feats for Lancashire in roses cricket but only one man, Higgs, has ever achieved the hat-trick against Yorkshire. The Staffordshire-born bowler did the trick at Leeds in 1968, and it is also recorded that the Reverend J. R. Napier had a four wickets without cost spell, way back in the days towards the close of the nineteenth century. No bowler has taken all ten Yorkshire wickets in a match to date, but A. G. Steel was on the verge of this remarkable achievement in 1878 when he had figures of 9-63 at Old Trafford. Three times the one and only Johnny Briggs dismissed eight roses batsmen in an innings, at Old Trafford in 1891 and 1892 and at Leeds in 1893. Mold, also, had his fair share of Yorkshire wickets and in 1890 he must have been a real thorn in the old enemy's side. At any rate he had 8-38 at Old Trafford and an even better 9-41 at Huddersfield. Dean, a left-hand spinner of the Briggs manner, also proved himself a destroyer of some consequence against Yorkshire with a magnificent haul of seventeen wickets at Liverpool in 1913. He had 9-62 in the first knock and 8-29 in

the second, and a year later Whitehead had 8-77 at Hull. Parkin's
best against Yorkshire was his 8-35 at Old Trafford in 1919 in a
match haul of 14-123, but McDonald seldom appeared to be at
his best on the most important occasions of the season. Coming
to more recent times, Tattersall had a superb 8-43 at Leeds in
1956 and Ramadhin took 8-121 in what was his first and last
roses game in 1964.

There is a difference of opinion between the two counties as
to when the roses matches really began, but Lancashire list 190
encounters with forty-two victories, sixty-three defeats and
eighty-five drawn games charting the course of matches that have
always been the biggest crowd-pullers of the summer. The
highest attendance on any one day at Old Trafford was in 1926
when 46,000 people watched the bank holiday play, and 38,906
of them paid for the privilege. Slow scoring and defensive
bowling may well be characteristic of these keenly-fought battles,
but they lose little in their appeal to the public and it is worth
noting that in these now fashionable days of Sunday League
cricket Lancashire and Yorkshire can still pull them in. Old
Trafford in 1969 and Leeds in 1971 prove the point. Spectators
were lining for admission at ten o'clock in the morning and play
was not due to start until 2 p.m.

On the field there is never anything but the keenness one
expects from rival cricketing counties. Gamesmanship is not unknown, but cheating is beyond the pale. Arguments about the
state of the pitch and the trend of the game are inevitable. The
players have their way and get on with the playing. The spectators hold forth and draw all and sundry into the argument. The
officials fraternize to a remarkable degree and nothing more indi-
cates the mutual admiration and understanding one has for the
other than the Yorkshire present of a special pennant to be flown
whenever the two sides clash, and the Lancashire decision to
honour Chairman Brian Sellers and Secretary John Nash with
honorary life membership when they retired in the course of last
winter.

Whatever the future may hold (and, for the first time since
the two counties first met, the 1972 clash at Old Trafford has to
withstand the competition of an England v Australia test at

Leeds), there can be no denying the importance and the value of these cricketing duels between Lancashire and Yorkshire. They are more than mere cricket matches. They are battles of wit between rival sportsmen fully aware of their responsibilities and reputations. In the past they have evoked admiration, despair, and tremendous public support. In the future they may have to fight hard for survival in a rapidly changing world – one in which sentiment and tradition counts for less and less. The cutting down of the county championship programme from twenty-four games to twenty might well be followed by a further reduction to sixteen in the face of fierce competition from the new one-day game, its sponsorship and its undoubted appeal to a public with far more choice of leisure-time pastimes.

Come what may, whatever happens to cricket there can be no devaluation of a roses game. It is something special, something that lifts itself higher than the rest, and it produces a quality of play not to be measured by any other standards. A batsman successful against Yorkshire is assured of Lancashire renown. A bowler who crashes his way through against White Rose batsmen is also sure of undying fame. It was always so, and it always will be so. When Lancashire meet Yorkshire it remains something personal to the two counties and the outcome matters more than usual, for the simple reason that it typifies a long and ancient battle for supremacy between two near neighbours. Neighbours who once shed blood in an attempt to settle their differences! Let the outsider scoff and the invader wonder. When Lancashire clash with Yorkshire no stranger can hope to understand what it is all about. It is purely and simply a question of blood being thicker than water.

29. INSURANCE FOR THE FUTURE

No cricket club, whatever its sphere of activity, can afford to ignore the future. Lancashire are well aware of this and they have given support to several organizations that can help them maintain the high standard of cricket now in evidence at Old

Trafford. More than twenty years ago, with former county chairman T. E. Burrows as the mainspring, the Lancashire Youth Cricket Council was formed to look after the youngsters who wanted to make progress in the game when they left school. Down the years this council, with Mr Burrows still at its head, has worked unceasingly to provide not only facilities for the young cricketer but also to establish and maintain a big pool of MCC-trained coaches available to spread the gospel in the many scattered cricketing communities that exist in the wide confines of the county. Lancashire was zoned for administration purposes in this respect and although not all the Youth Council aims have been achieved it remains a valuable link between the known and the unknown in the cricketing sphere. Courses for coaches are regular features of the council's work and so are training sessions for umpires and groundsmen. Its link with the schoolboy cricketer is strong and its liaison with the Lancashire Schools Cricket Association, of which, incidentally, Mr Burrows is president, assures that there is no great wastage of talent or enthusiasm, through losing touch with cricket, between the vital stage of a boy leaving school and finding himself employment. The council's meetings are usually held at Old Trafford and the county club's annual donation is money well spent inasmuch as it enables an organization of keen and hard-working officials to maintain and strengthen the ties between the highest and the lowest in the game.

The schoolboy cricketer of Lancashire has always been well catered for and none have worked harder in this direction than one of the county's newest vice-presidents. Herbert Thomas is the Grand Old Man of Lancashire cricket. Well in his eighties, this long-since retired Manchester schoolmaster was not only a founder member of the Lancashire Schools Cricket Association but also its first secretary, and for over thirty years Mr Thomas has devoted all his time and energy to the betterment of cricket in the schools. In addition to his demanding duties with the Lancashire Association he was also a leading figure behind the formation of the English Schools Cricket Association and his work for the Manchester Association was no less important. Awarded the MBE for his services to the cricketing cause, he has served with such great distinction that Mr Thomas is now the holder of a unique position in cricket – that of Honorary Secretary Emeritus to the Lancashire Association – and he follows their activities with a keen eye and alert mind. In an advisory capacity his services are still highly valued and nothing indicated the appreciation of the Lancashire County Cricket Club better than their desire to add his name to the many notables who have enjoyed the office of vice-presidency at Old Trafford. It was a sincere as well as a wise gesture for it is Mr Thomas and the schools people he enthusiastically led for so many years who do the spadework for Lancashire. The schoolboy player of today is the county cricketer of a few years hence, and in Lancashire he has never lacked encouragement. It is a tribute to Mr Thomas and his kind that the schoolboy player now enjoys the privilege of cricket at representative level and that it reaches from town to international heights, with tours abroad now part and parcel of the schools sporting curriculum.

Taking over where the schools leave off is the Lancashire Cricket Federation, an organization comprising most of the leagues and clubs in the county, founded in 1947 and inspired by another enthusiastic cricket lover in the person of Albert E. Hall, a Bolton man who was a cricketer of only moderate ability but a lover of the game and an administrator second to none. Mr Hall saw the necessity for the formation of a body to safeguard the interest of the Saturday afternoon clubs and their players. He realized that individually they could achieve little but that collectively they had a chance to exert influence and improve their lot. Although not taking an active part in the federation's affairs, the Lancashire County Cricket Club has always been at hand to lend assistance. Financially its annual donation is still one of the most important sources of the federation's income and Old Trafford is one of its committee's regular meeting places.

From the Lancashire headquarters, too, has come two of the federation's presidents, in Major Rupert Howard who held office until his death, and ever since by Mr A. J. Leggatt, a member of the county committee and a former club cricketer of repute. One of the federation's earliest efforts was their successful battle on behalf of the Cheetham Cricket Club when they went to the

House of Lords to decide a delicate question of liability over the famous 'Six Hit' case, when a big-hitting batsman created havoc by his bombardment of property bordering on to the ground with his ferocious hitting. Losing the battle for damages in the lower courts, the federation enlisted the aid of Lancashire and then Lords in successfully challenging the decision in the highest court of all and setting a precedent for any other similar case of cricketing transgression.

Today most of the federation's activities are devoted to the building of a Youth Side each summer, and from the ranks of this teenage representative team have sprung nearly every young player of note in the county's cricketing history. It is no easy task organizing and sustaining a series of trials, followed by representative games at home and on tour, but the Lancashire Federation Youth Team is an annual source of much benefit to the county and Old Trafford's coaches, Norman Oldfield and John Savage, pay ready tribute to the men behind the scheme.

Two of these men behind the scenes, both enthusiastic schoolteachers, are Jim Gledhill and Doug Cameron, and they deserve to be ranked as talent-spotters extraordinary. Their keen eyes, persuasive tongues and enthusiastic endeavours discover and encourage an annual batch of promising young cricketers without which the county club could not survive. It is organizations and workers like these which do much to smooth the way for the parent club; and the formation of the new Lancashire Cricket Association, the essential link between the village green and Lord's, now completes the united front so essential in a county's cricketing orbit. With the county chairman, Cedric Rhoades, at the head, the new association represents every shade of cricket opinion and thought in Lancashire, and although progress towards the desired goal of complete unity must of necessity be slow, there can be no doubting the earnest attempts now being made in this direction. Given time, good will and understanding of one another's problems, Old Trafford will soon be the headquarters of one of the strongest and most progressive cricketing bodies in the country. It was not always so!

175

Those vital statistics

Averages are often said to be the curse of cricket. Yet the keeping of the records is a vital aspect of the game and Lancashire, like most other county clubs, have been well served in this respect. Their annual yearbook is a veritable mine of information on such matters and the section devoted to 'vital statistics' is often the cause of arguments . . . and the means of settling many more. It may well be asserted that such elegant batsmen as Reggie Spooner and Charlie Hallows needed no figures to emphasize their class and that the great Sydney Barnes and the ever-accurate Brian Statham proved their ability without recourse to averages or the record book. That may well be so, but there can be no denying the value of figures and the pleasure that can be gained by turning back the pages and reliving the successes of the past. Here, then, are listed the major achievements of the batsmen and the bowlers who have contributed so much to the story of Lancashire cricket for more than a century:

HIGHEST INDIVIDUAL SCORES FOR LANCASHIRE

424	A. C. MacLaren, v. Somerset (Taunton)	1895
322	E. Paynter, v. Sussex (Hove)	1937
300	F. Watson, v. Surrey (Old Trafford)	1928
295	J. T. Tyldesley, v. Kent (Old Trafford)	1906
291	E. Paynter, v. Hampshire (Southampton)	1938
272	J. T. Tyldesley, v. Derbyshire (Chesterfield) ...	1919
266	W. Place, v. Oxford University (Oxford)	1947
266	E. Paynter, v. Essex (Old Trafford)	1937
256	E. Tyldesley, v. Warwickshire (Old Trafford) ...	1930
253	J. T. Tyldesley, v. Kent (Canterbury)	1914
251	C. Washbrook, v. Surrey (Old Trafford)	1947
250	J. T. Tyldesley, v. Notts (Nottingham)	1905

HIGHEST INDIVIDUAL SCORES AGAINST LANCASHIRE

315	T. Hayward, for Surrey (Oval)	1898
282	A. Sandham, for Surrey (Old Trafford)	1928
274	G. Davidson, for Derbyshire (Old Trafford) ...	1896
271	W. R. Hammond, for Gloucestershire (Bristol) ...	1938
264	W. R. Hammond, for Gloucestershire (Liverpool)	1932
260	R. Subba Row, for Northants (Northampton) ...	1955
260	A. P. F. Chapman, for Kent (Maidstone)	1927
250	W. R. Hammond, for Glos (Old Trafford) ...	1925

BATSMEN WHO HAVE SCORED 10,000
RUNS FOR LANCASHIRE

	For Lancashire			All First-Class Matches	
	Runs	*Aver.*		*Runs*	*Aver.*
E. Tyldesley ...	34,222	45.20	...	38,874	45.46
J. T. Tyldesley ...	31,949	41.38	...	37,897	40.66
C. Washbrook ...	27,863	42.14	...	34,101	42.67
H. Makepeace ...	25,207	36.37	...	25,799	36.23
F. Watson	22,833	37.06	...	23,596	36.98
J. Iddon	21,975	37.05	...	22,681	36.76
J. Sharp	21,815	30.89	...	22,715	31.11
K. J. Grieves ...	20,802	33.39	...	22,454	33.66
C. Hallows	20,142	39.72	...	20,926	40.24
A. Wharton ...	17,921	33.55	...	21,796	32.24
G. Pullar	16,853	35.18	...	21,528	35.34
E. Paynter	16,555	41.59	...	20,075	42.26
A. C. MacLaren ...	15,735	33.26	...	21,959	34.04
J. L. Hopwood ...	15,519	30.05	...	15,548	29.90
A. Ward	15,264	30.77	...	17,783	30.08
G. A. Edrich ...	14,730	34.74	...	15,600	34.82
W. Place	14,605	36.69	...	15,609	35.63
J. T. Ikin	14,327	37.70	...	17,968	36.81
J. D. Bond	11,005	27.10	...	11,018	27.00
J. Briggs	10,617	18.99	...	13,983	18.19
P. T. Marner ...	10,312	29.21	...	17,513	28.33
A. N. Hornby ...	10,294	23.88	...	15,798	23.72

BOWLERS WHO HAVE TAKEN 500 WICKETS
FOR LANCASHIRE

| | For Lancashire | | | All First-Class Matches | |
	Wkts.	Aver.		Wkts.	Aver.
J. B. Statham ...	1,816	15.12	...	2,260	16.36
J. Briggs	1,688	15.65	...	2,201	15.99
A. Mold	1,541	15.13	...	1,673	15.54
R. K. Tyldesley ...	1,449	16.65	...	1,509	17.21
A. Watson	1,279	13.47	...	1,338	13.46
H. Dean	1,267	18.01	...	1,301	18.14
R. Tattersall ...	1,168	17.39	...	1,369	18.04
E. A. McDonald	1,053	20.96	...	1,395	20.76
K. Higgs	1,033	22.90	...	1,165	23.12
R. Pollard	1,015	22.14	...	1,122	22.56
F. M. Sibbles ...	932	22.11	...	940	22.43
M. J. Hilton ...	926	18.81	...	1,006	19.41
C. H. Parkin ...	901	16.12	...	1,048	17.58
L. Cook	821	21.36	...	839	21.20
W. R. Cuttell ...	760	19.59	...	792	19.59
R. G. Barlow ...	726	13.59	...	933	14.52
T. Greenhough ...	707	21.98	...	751	22.37
W. Brearley ...	690	18.70	...	844	19.31
W. Huddleston ...	674	17.55	...	685	17.57
J. L. Hopwood ...	672	22.18	...	673	22.45
W. E. Phillipson ...	545	24.78	...	555	24.72
J. Iddon	533	26.66	...	551	26.90

HIGHEST INNINGS TOTALS AGAINST EACH TEAM

546	v. Derbyshire (Old Trafford)	1898
510	v. Essex (Clacton)	1947
564-9	v. Glamorgan (Old Trafford)	1938
474-3	v. Gloucestershire (Liverpool)	1903
676-7	v. Hampshire (Old Trafford)	1911
531	v. Kent (Old Trafford)	1906
590	v. Leicestershire (Leicester)	1899
484-8	v. Middlesex (Old Trafford)	1926
528-4	v. Northamptonshire (Old Trafford)	1928
627	v. Nottinghamshire (Nottingham)	1905
801	v. Somerset (Taunton)	1895
588-4	v. Surrey (Old Trafford)	1928
640-8	v. Sussex (Hove)	1937

526	v. Warwickshire (Birmingham)	... ...	1920
592-4	v. Worcestershire (Worcester)	... ...	1929
509-9	v. Yorkshire (Old Trafford) ...	... ...	1926
346	v. Australians (Old Trafford)	... ...	1961
445-6	v. South Africans (Old Trafford) ...	... ...	1924
405	v. West Indies (Old Trafford)	... ...	1923
487	v. New Zealanders (Liverpool)	... ...	1931
436-7	v. Indians (Blackpool)	... ...	1959
324	v. Pakistanis (Old Trafford)	... ...	1954
512-8	v. Oxford University (Oxford)	... ...	1947
470-4	v. Cambridge University (Old Trafford)	...	1960
365-6	v. MCC (Old Trafford)	... ...	1957

HIGHEST INNINGS TOTAL
BY EACH TEAM AGAINST LANCASHIRE

577	by Derbyshire (Old Trafford)	... ...	1896
559-9	by Essex (Leyton)	... ...	1904
425	by Glamorgan (Old Trafford)	... ...	1938
561	by Gloucestershire (Bristol)	... ...	1938
487	by Hampshire (Liverpool)	... ...	1901
479	by Kent (Canterbury)	... ...	1906
493	by Leicestershire (Leicester)	... ...	1910
503-3	by Middlesex (Lord's)	... ...	1914
517-9	by Northamptonshire (Northampton)	... ...	1955
504-5	by Nottinghamshire (Old Trafford)	... ...	1949
561	by Somerset (Bath)	... ...	1901
634	by Surrey (Oval)	... ...	1898
485	by Sussex (Old Trafford)	... ...	1903
532-4	by Warwickshire (Birmingham)	... ...	1901
492	by Worcestershire (Old Trafford)	... ...	1906
590	by Yorkshire (Bradford)	... ...	1887
548-6	by Australians (Old Trafford)	... ...	1961
429	by South Africans (Old Trafford)	... ...	1907
454-7	by West Indies (Old Trafford)	... ...	1950
410-9	by New Zealanders (Liverpool)	... ...	1931
493	by Indians (Liverpool)	... ...	1932
303	by Pakistanis (Old Trafford) ...	... ...	1962
419-8	by Oxford University (Oxford)	... ...	1960
416	by Cambridge University (Liverpool)	... ...	1957
404	by MCC (Lord's)	... ...	1897

LOWEST TOTAL AGAINST EACH TEAM

25	v. Derbyshire (Old Trafford)	1871
73	v. Essex (Old Trafford)	1957
49	v. Glamorgan (Liverpool)	1924
45	v. Gloucestershire (Preston)	1936
54	v. Hampshire (Portsmouth)	1937
61	v. Kent (Canterbury)	1884
73	v. Leicestershire (Leicester)	1935
63	v. Middlesex (Lord's)	1891
80	v. Northamptonshire (Old Trafford)	1965
37	v. Nottinghamshire (Liverpool)	1907
48	v. Somerset (Old Trafford)	1892
27	v. Surrey (Old Trafford)	1958
55	v. Sussex (Old Trafford)	1892
70	v. Warwickshire (Old Trafford)	1955
55	v. Worcestershire (Worcester)	1965
30	v. Yorkshire (Holbeck)	1868
28	v. Australians (Liverpool)	1896
90	v. South Africans (Blackpool)	1960
79	v. West Indies (Old Trafford)	1957
229	v. New Zealanders (Old Trafford)	1927
68	v. Indians (Old Trafford)	1952
98	v. Pakastanis (Old Trafford)	1954
82	v. Oxford University (Oxford)	1958
65	v. Cambridge University (Cambridge)	1907
49	v. MCC (Lord's)	1880

LOWEST INNINGS TOTAL
BY EACH TEAM AGAINST LANCASHIRE

37	by Derbyshire (Chesterfield)	1922
37	by Derbyshire (Old Trafford)	1923
59	by Essex (Liverpool)	1931
22	by Glamorgan (Liverpool)	1924
33	by Gloucestershire (Liverpool)	1888
37	by Hampshire (Old Trafford)	1900
38	by Kent (Maidstone)	1881
33	by Leicestershire (Leicester)	1925
69	by Middlesex (Lord's)	1933

48	by Northamptonshire (Northampton)	1922
35	by Nottinghamshire (Nottingham)	1895
31	by Somerset (Old Trafford)	1894
33	by Surrey (Oval)	1873
24	by Sussex (Old Trafford)	1890
49	by Warwickshire (Birmingham)	1896
48	by Worcestershire (Worcester)	1910
33	by Yorkshire (Leeds)	1924
66	by Australians (Old Trafford)	1888
44	by South Africans (Liverpool)	1912
108	by West Indies (Old Trafford)	1928
104	by New Zealanders (Old Trafford)	1965
85	by Indians (Old Trafford)	1911
219	by Pakistanis (Old Trafford)	1954
58	by Oxford University (Liverpool)	1887
31	by Cambridge University (Old Trafford)	1882
30	by MCC (Lord's)	1886

RECORD PARTNERSHIPS FOR EACH WICKET

1st	368	A. C. MacLaren and R. H. Spooner, v. Gloucestershire, at Aigburth	1903
2nd	371	F. Watson and E. Tyldesley, v. Surrey, at Old Trafford	1928
3rd	306	E. Paynter and N. Oldfield, v. Hampshire, at Southampton	1938
4th	324	A. C. MacLaren and J. T. Tyldesley, v. Notts. at Nottingham	1904
5th	235	N. Oldfield and A. Nutter, v. Notts, at Old Trafford	1939
6th	278	J. Iddon and H. R. W. Butterworth, v. Sussex, at Old Trafford	1932
7th	245	A. H. Hornby and J. Sharp, v. Leicestershire, at Old Trafford	1912
8th	150	A. Ward and C. R. Hartley, v. Leicestershire, at Leicester	1900
9th	142	L. O. S. Poidevin and A. Kermode, v. Sussex, at Eastbourne	1907
10th	173	J. Briggs and R. Pilling, v. Surrey, at Aigburth	1885

1,000 RUNS IN MAY

C. Hallows 1928 1,000 runs in May equalled W. G. Grace's record, as W. R. Hammond had done the previous season.

1,000 RUNS IN JULY

E. Tyldesley in 1926 and C. Washbrook in 1946 achieved this in all first-class matches.

Index